COUNTRY KITCHEN COLLECTION

Silver Hills Guest House

"fantastically delicious & nutritious vegetarian meals"

ISBN 1-878726-20-X

**Library of Congress Catalog Card Number
91-76560**

Printed in the United States of America

Family Health Publications
8777 E. Musgrove Hwy.
Sunfield, MI. 48890

INTRODUCTION

Some of the most rapid changes in the lifestyle of mankind have taken place since the turn of the century. We have come a long way from the rural farming community to the modern computer-orientated city. Not only have our clothes, houses and entertainment changed, but also our eating habits and health. Since 1900 sugar consumption has gone up over 200%. Fat consumption has almost doubled and the use of grains has dropped by half. The local country store has changed into a chain of supermarkets with thousands of prepared foods ready for the eating. With all these improvements you would expect that our health would be improving, but actually the results are just the opposite. Medical expenditures over the past 20 years have reached an all-time high and many diseases are a result of our health habits.

SILVER HILLS GUEST HOUSE, built in the mountains of British Columbia, is dedicated to teaching guests how to regain their health according to natures laws. We use eight natural doctors, **sunlight, rest, exercise, water, good food, temperance, fresh air,** and **trust in God** to assist nature in the battle with disease. During the twenty-one days that a guest spends with us, we serve them a wide variety of vegetarian foods. **COUNTRY KITCHEN COLLECTION** is an outgrowth of the menus we serve each day at our table for the benefit of our health guests.

In **COUNTRY KITCHEN COLLECTION** we have tried to make the recipes as tasty and nutritious as possible. When it comes to eating we all have personal preferences; some have allergies, and other have convictions. These menus and recipes are not meant to establish rules or regulations but only to offer you assistance in the art of cookery. The menus in this book are suggestions only. Change according to your family's tastes, desires, and availability. Plan your menus to get a variety each week. Choose from these six different categories, Beans, Pastas, Rice, Soups, Patties, Casseroles and Loaves. You will find that this will save you a lot of time and frustration.

"Let not the work of cooking be looked upon as a sort of slavery. What would become of those in our world if all who are engaged in cooking should give up their work with the flimsy excuse that it is not sufficiently dignified? Cooking may be regarded as less desirable than some other lines of work but in reality it is a science in value above all other sciences. Thus God regards the preparation of healthful food. He places a high estimate on those who do faithful service in preparing wholesome, palatable food. The one who understands the art of properly preparing food, and who uses this knowledge is worthy of higher commendation than those engaged in any other line of work. This talent should be regarded as equal in value to ten talents; for its right use has much to do with keeping the human organism in health. Because so inseparably connected with life and health, it is the most valuable of all gifts." Counsels on Diet and Foods, page 25.

NOTE: Some recipes will contain a word or title in capital letters. Look up this word or title in the index. This represents a recipe within a recipe. For example, VEGETARIAN OMELET, on page 17, calls for CHICKEN STYLE SEASONING. After looking in the index we find this seasoning on page 214.

INTRODUCTION

TOP OF THE MORNING - BREAKFASTS

CATCHIE CASSEROLES

PLEASING PATTIES

3

FAMILY FUN

ICE BOX INCIDENTALS

PANTRY BASICS

ARTICLES

INDEX

Menus & Recipes

Top of the Morning

THIS SPACE FOR YOUR NOTES & RECIPES

_____

_____

_____

_____

_____

_____

_____

_____

_____

_____

_____

_____

_____

_____

_____

BREAKFAST

"Breakfast?"- Half the population would say, "I hate breakfast. I can't stand getting up that early. Besides, do I really need it?"

Let's look at our present eating habits. A usual quick, light breakfast of something sweet: a normal coffee break; a light lunch; probably another coffee break; and home for a main meal called supper, (or dinner) and maybe a follow-up evening snack. Even with keeping the breakfast and light lunch to a minimum, we are still gaining weight, so who needs breakfast? The night life with TV entertainment and electric lights make even the thought of food before 10 a.m. painful.

Actually the most important meal of the day is breakfast. Those who eat a hearty breakfast have fewer accidents and rate higher on performance tests on production. School children get better grades and have less of the problems associated with blood sugar imbalances. After a night of rest the stomach is better prepared than ever to digest. The brain also needs the nutrients to be alert and ready for the day's activities.

The problems are created by eating a hearty supper and finally going to bed. First of all, since the body does not need food at that time, the food is stored. These storage areas become overcrowded and begin to bulge. In the morning when we need the food, we grab something quick and sweet for energy and follow it up through the day with more sweet snacks that add to our weight problem.

A good breakfast satisfies our body needs, and if made from whole grains will give us energy right through to lunch without morning blood sugar slumps. The other problem created by a big supper is even more serious than being over weight. Food eaten and not digested before going to bed keeps the digestive organs working on into the sleeping hours. Our sleep is not as deep and refreshing as it should be, and consequently the cycle of the wearisome, hurried mornings results with tired brains and nerves. Try eating a light supper and a better breakfast.

One lady is said to have lost 50 pounds. This was not done by changing her diet but by eating her supper for breakfast.

Top of the Morning

OPENERS
Basket of Bananas, Oranges, Apples

BREAKFAST SPECIAL
French Toast - Sunflower or Garbanzo

FROM GRANDMOTHER'S CELLAR
Hot Apple Sauce
Nut Raisin Spread
Pear Cream, Peanut Butter or Corn Butter

FRENCH TOAST #1

1/2 c. sunflower seeds, cashews or almonds
2 1/4 c. water
2 Tbs. honey
1 Tbs. vanilla or maple flavoring
1/2 tsp. salt
2 c. oats

Blend all ingredients until smooth. Pour into a bowl. Dip about 12 slices of bread in this batter. 1) Place on greased cookie sheet. Bake at 400 for 10 minutes. Reduce heat to 350 until toast is nicely browned. May want to put under broiler to brown top quickly at end. 2) Or fry on nonstick griddle or fry pan.

FRENCH TOAST #2

1 c. soaked garbanzo beans
2/3 c. water
1 c. MILLET or ALMOND MILK
1/2 tsp. salt
1 1/2 tsp. vanilla or maple flavor
2 Tbs. brown sugar, optional
6 slices of bread

Soak 1/2 c. dried garbanzo beans in 2 c. of water for at least 6 hours. Drain. Blend beans with water from the recipe until smooth. Add remaining ingredients. Pour into bowl. Dip the bread and bake on greased nonstick skillet or bake in oven at 375 turning when browned.

NUT RAISIN SPREAD

1 c. cashews
1 c. almonds
1 Tbs. grated lemon peel
1/2 tsp. ground coriander
1 c. orange juice
1 c. raisins

Place nuts in food processor. Grind until a paste forms. Mix in remaining ingredients. May add all ingredients to food processor after grinding nuts if desired. Makes 36-1 Tbs. servings.

PEAR CREAM see page 196

CORN BUTTER see page 198

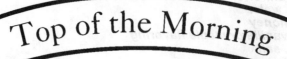

Top of the Morning

OPENERS
Oranges & Bananas

BREAKFAST SPECIAL
**Granola (No Sugar Granola, Almond Crunch,
or Favorite Granola)
Favorite Milk**

FROM GRANDMOTHER'S CELLAR
Peaches/Pears Combination

BREAD BASKET
Cobbler Biscuits

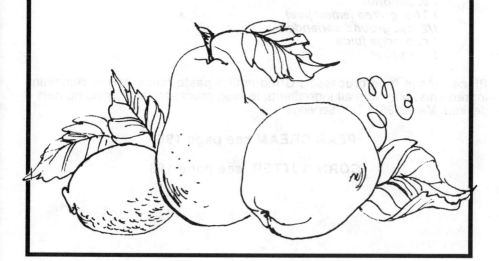

NO SUGAR GRANOLA

1 c. dates
1/2 c. water
2 ripe bananas
1 1/2 tsp. salt
1 c. coconut
1 c. chopped nuts
1/2 c. sunflower seeds
10 c. rolled oats

Simmer dates in water until soft. Blend smooth with next 2 ingredients. Mix together all ingredients. Spread on cookie sheets 1/2 inch thick. Bake at 200 for 90 min. stirring every 30 min.
Variation: 1 c. rye or barley flakes may be substituted for 2 c. oats.

ALMOND CRUNCH GRANOLA

1 c. boiling water
1 c. dates, chopped
3 med. apples, cored and chopped
1/2 tsp. salt
1 tsp. vanilla
1 c. almonds, ground dry in blender
1 c. coconut
1/2 c. cornmeal
1 c. wheat flakes or oats
8 c. rolled oats

Simmer until tender first three ingredients; then blend smooth with salt and vanilla. Combine with almonds and coconut. When cool, stir in remaining ingredients. Crumble mixture over large cookie sheets. Bake at 250. Stir every 20 to 30 minutes. After 1 hour, reduce heat to 200. Bake until dry, about 1-2 hours.

FAVORITE GRANOLA

8 c. rolled oats
1 c. coconut
1 c. sunflower seeds
1 c. chopped almonds
1/2 c. brown sugar or sucanut
1 tsp. salt
1/2 c. PEAR MILK or water
2 Tbs. vanilla
2 Tbs. maple

Mix wet and dry ingredients separately then combine. Crumble and spread on cookie sheets. Bake at 275, stirring every 3 min. for about 1 12 to 2 hours, until lightly browned and dry.

Top of the Morning

OPENERS
Golden Apples

BREAKFAST SPECIAL
Waffles - (3 choices of recipes)

FROM GRANDMOTHER'S CELLAR
Thickened Blueberries or Fresh Sliced Peaches
Blueberry Orange Sauce
Strawberries & Crushed Pineapple
Pear Cream
Peanut Butter or Corn Butter

COCONUT OAT WAFFLES

8 c. oats
1 c. ground millet or cornmeal
1/2 c. coconut
2 tsp. salt
2 tsp. vanilla
1 Tbs. maple flavoring
1/2 c. almonds, ground fine (optional)
10-12 c. water

Mix first four ingredients together. Blend flavorings and nuts with part of the water untill smooth. Mix with rest of water and pour over oat mixture. Let stand several hours or overnight. Blend well, (may need to add more water). Pour into hot waffle iron. Baie 10-12 minutes. Yields 12 waffles. Use any fruit, or warm or cold thickened fruit or "Jams" to put on top of waffles.

THE WAFFLE PERFECT

2 1/2 c. oats
3/4 c. cornmeal
3/4 c. whole wheat flour
1/3 c. nuts blended in 1 tsp. salt & 1 c. water

Stir in 4-4 1/2 c. water. Blend thoroughly. Batter will be thin as this makes a lighter waffle. Serve with 1 c. thickened grape juice, 1 c. applesauce, 1 c. blueberries.

SESAME-OAT WAFFLES

1 c. sesame seeds raw
1 1/2 c. quick oats
1 1/2 c. cornmeal
1 tsp. salt
4 c. water
2 Tbs. olive oil, optional

Blend the seeds with part of the water. Add remaining ingredients and water to make a good batter. Bake in hot waffle iron.

STRAWBERRIES & CRUSHED PINEAPPLE

To thicken strawberries:
Partially thaw berries, strain out juice. Bring juice to boil add arrowroot or cornstarch water mixture to thicken. Add honey if necessary. Add this thickened juice back to strawberries and add 1 small tin crushed pineapple.

BLUEBERRY ORANGE SAUCE see page 197

PEAR CREAM see page 196

Top of the Morning

OPENERS
Orange Slices

BREAKFAST SPECIAL
Scrambled Tofu (Baco Bits-optional, or Omelet)

FROM GRANDMOTHER'S CELLAR
Side dish of chunky Apple Sauce (may wish brown beans here for a cowboy special)

BREAD BASKET
June's Whole Wheat Bread/Corn Butter
Raspberry Jam or Tomato slices

VEGETARIAN OMELET

1/2 c. water
1/2 c. rice flour or oat flour
1/4 c. cashews
1 lb. tofu
1 tsp. salt
1 tsp. onion powder
1 tsp. garlic powder
1/8 tsp. turmeric for color, optional
1 Tbs. CHICKEN STYLE SEASONING
2 Tbs. nutritional yeast flakes
1 tsp. lecithin, optional

Combine all ingredients and blend. Grease nonstick skillet, preheat and pour in 1/2 of omelet mixture. Cover and cook over medium low heat for 10 min. or until lightly browned. Loosen around edges and slide out on plate. Turn fry pan upside down over plate. Invert so the uncooked side of omelet is on the bottom of pan. Cover and fry 10 min. Allow to set for a few minutes. This makes two.

SCRAMBLED TOFU

1 lb. tofu
1/2 tsp. garlic salt
1 Tbs. parsley flakes or dried chives
1 1/2 Tbs. CHICKEN STYLE SEASONING
1 tsp. onion powder
1 tsp. Magi or soy sauce
1/4 tsp. turmeric, optional
1/4 tsp. salt, optional

Lightly grease nonstick skillet. Crumble rinsed tofu on skillet. Sprinkle seasonings on tofu. Add any of the following options: mushrooms, onions, soy sauce, paprika. Stir and let brown turning occasionally. Serve on platter, sprinkle with baco bites if desired, or with KETCHUP.

GRANDMA'S OLD FASHIONED RASPBERRY JAM

Method #1 - Using no sugar
3 c. raspberries, fresh or frozen
5 rings dried pineapple
Pineapple or orange juice as needed for consistency, especially if it's fresh raspberries.
Rinse dried pineapple in water to remove any sulphur. Cut dried pineapple into small pieces. Combine all ingredients and let sit until pineapple is soft. If using frozen fruit, do night by setting pineapple in bottom of bowl and put frozen fruit on top of pineapple. Next morning stir and then blend until smooth. Add liquid if necessary.

Variation: See page 199. This recipe uses some sugar.

JUNE'S WHOLE WHEAT BREAD see page 220

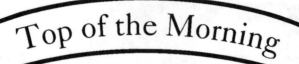

Top of the Morning

OPENERS
Oranges & Fresh Berries

BREAKFAST SPECIAL
Seven Grain Cereal
Favorite Milk

FROM GRANDMOTHER'S CELLAR
Cherries-canned without sugar

BREAD BASKET
Apple Burritos

SEVEN GRAIN CEREAL

1 1/2 c. Seven Grain Cereal
2 qts. water
1 tsp. salt

Bring water and salt to a boil in a covered saucepan. Stir in cereal. Cover. Return to a very light boil. Cook 1-2 hours. Do not stir while cooking or it will badly stick or burn.

APPLE BURRITOS

8 apples, peeled and cored
1/3 c. water
1/4 c. dates, chopped
1/4 c. raisins
1/4 tsp. maple flavoring
1 tsp. vanilla

Cook apples and dates in water until soft. Add remaining ingredients. Mix well. Roll in tortilla shell and place in baking dish. Cover with glaze. Bake at 350 for 30-40 minutes.

GLAZE

2 c. apple juice
2 Tbs. cornstarch or arrowroot powder
1/2 tsp. lemon juice
1/4 tsp. coriander, optional
1/8 tsp. cardamon, optional

Mix ingredients together and cook over medium heat until lightly thickened. Use on waffles or crepes. May use frozen concentrate for apple juice.

TORTILLAS

2 c. whole wheat flour
1/2 c. white flour
3/4 c. hot water
1/2 tsp. salt
1/4 c. applesauce

Mix flours together. Combine hot water, salt and applesauce. Add the liquid to the dry ingredients. Mix well. Divide dough into small balls; roll thin, fry on ungreased skillet.

MILKS see page 195

CANNED CHERRIES see page 209

Top of the Morning

OPENERS
Oranges & Kiwi Slices

BREAKFAST SPECIAL
Oatmeal - (LeRoy's Special, Baked, Whole Oats)
Millet Milk

FROM GRANDMOTHER'S CELLAR
Frozen or Canned Stewed Plums

BREAD BASKET
Danish Sweet Rolls
Peanut Butter & Apricot Jam

BAKED OATMEAL

3 c. oats
1 1/2 c. dates or raisins
3/4 c. coconut1 tsp. salt
1 Tbs. vanilla
4 1/2 c. liquid, choose from: water, soy milk, tofu milk or MILK
from beverage section

Layer first three ingredients in an 8 x 12 pan in the order given. Mix salt and vanilla with enough milk or water to cover the oat mixture. Bake at 350 for 1 hour. May let stand overnight before baking.

Variation: Use pineapple, orange or apple juice.

LEROY'S SPECIAL

2 c. water
1 c. oats
1/4 tsp. salt
1 Tbs. flaxseed
1/4 c. raisins

Bring water and salt to a boil in a covered saucepan. Stir in remaining ingredients. Cover. Lightly boil 30-60 minutes. Do not stir while cooking.

WHOLE OATS

1 3/4 c. oat groats
4 c. water
1 tsp. salt

Bring water and salt to a boil in a covered saucepan. Stir in oats. Cover. Lightly boil 1-2 hours

STEWED PRUNES

Frozen stewed prunes are so nice. Simply pit and freeze plums. When ready to use, heat in kettle with small amount of water. Bring to boil, simmer until nicely stewed. Add desired amount of honey. May use frozen grape juice concentrate in place of water and honey.

MILLET MILK see page 195

DANISH SWEET ROLLS see page 225

APRICOT JAM see page 200

Top of the Morning

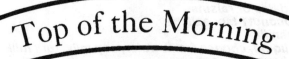

OPENERS
Grapefruit Halves

BREAKFAST SPECIAL
Whole Wheat Crepes

FROM GRANDMOTHER'S CELLAR
Strawberry Jam
Pear Cream
Cera Jel Jam
Maple Syrup or Melted Honey with Maple Flavoring

WHOLE WHEAT CREPES

1 c. rolled oats
1 c. whole wheat flour
2 c. milk; soy, tofu, MILLET or nut
1 dried pineapple ring, optional

Soak all ingredients above overnight in cool place to develop gluten. Just before using, put in blender and add the ingredients in Part 2 below.

1 c. milk, approximately
1 tsp. salt
vanilla to taste
maple flavoring to taste

Blend to consistency of thin cream. Put 1-2 Tbs. of mixture onto heated, nonstick skillet to thoroughly cover bottom and immediately tip pan in a circular motion to spread evenly. Cook until edges begin to brown. Top side needs to be dry. Turn to brown other side if desired. Tip out immediately onto a flat plate. Keep stacking crepes on top of each other. Fill with fresh fruit or top with canned fruit.

STRAWBERRY JAM

2 c. fresh or frozen strawberries
4-5 rings of dried pineapple
pineapple or orange juice as needed for consistency

Rinse dried pineapple in water to remove any sulphur. Cut dried pineapple into small pieces. Combine all ingredients and let set until diced pineapple is soft. Blend in blender until smooth. It may not need any juice if the strawberries have enough liquid.

MAPLE SYRUP

1 c. water
1 Tbs. arrowroot
1 c. honey
1 tsp. maple flavoring

Mix arrowroot and a little water into a paste. Add remaining water. Cook, stirring constantly, until clear and thick. Stir in honey and maple flavoring. Makes two cups.

CERA JEL JAMS see page 200

PEAR CREAM see page 196

Top of the Morning

OPENERS
Fresh Fruit Salad

BREAKFAST SPECIAL
Barley Flakes or Barley Pudding
Raisins
Favorite Milk

FROM GRANDMOTHER'S CELLAR
Raspberries
(See canning without sugar)

BREAD BASKET
Date or Raisin Rolls
Orange Date Syrup

BARLEY FLAKES

1 c. barley flakes
2 c. water
1/2 tsp. salt

Bring water and salt to a boil in a covered saucepan. Stir in barley. Cover. Lightly boil 45-60 min. Do not stir while cooking.

BARLEY PUDDING

1 c. slivered, raw almonds
1 c. pearl barley
12 c. water
2 c. chopped, dried fruit: apricots, prunes, etc.
1 1/2 c. raisins
1/3 c. honey
1-2 tsp. salt
1/2 tsp. ground coriander

Spread slivered almonds in a shallow pan and toast until brown. In 4 qt. pan, combine barley and 8 c. water. Lightly boil, uncovered, for 30 minutes. Add chopped fruit, raisins, and remaining water. Continue cooking for another 30 minutes until thick. Add honey, salt and coriander and cook, stirring, 5-10 minutes longer. Remove from heat and sprinkle almonds on top. Can be made day before and warmed.

RAISIN ROLLS

2 c. rinsed raisins
2 c. water
2 tsp. maple flavoring
1 Tbs. arrowroot or cornstarch

Mix all together in a saucepan. Lightly boil, stirring about 5 minutes. Use as filling for sweet rolls.

ORANGE DATE SYRUP

1 c. boiling water
1 c. pitted dates
3/4 c. frozen orange juice concentrate

Simmer water and dates together until soft. Remove from heat and add orange juice concentrate. Whiz in blender, pour into container and store in refrigerator.

Top of the Morning

OPENERS
Orange & Kiwi Slices or any fresh fruit in season

BREAKFAST SPECIAL
Oat Bran
Favorite Milk

FROM GRANDMOTHER'S CELLAR
Peaches

BREAD BASKET
Baked Apples

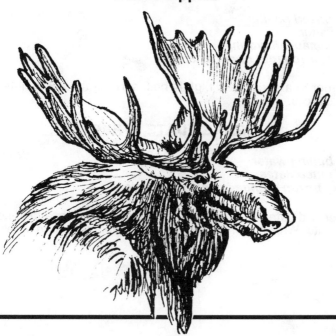

OAT BRAN

2 c. water
2/3 c. oat bran
1/2 tsp. salt

Bring water and salt to boil in a covered saucepan. Add oat bran slowly to avoid lumping. Reduce heat and cook 1-2 minutes stirring often. Will thicken as cools.

BAKED APPLES

Apples
Dates
Raisins
Brown sugar
Spices, (such as coriander, anise, and/or cardamon)
Whole wheat bread dough or pie pastry

Take whole apples, core and stuff centers with dates, raisins, brown sugar and spices. Wrap in bread dough or pie pastry that has been rolled out about 1/4-1/2 inch thick. Let rise for 10-15 min. Bake 350° for 45 min. Warm before serving.

CANNED PEACHES see page 209

MILK see page 195

Top of the Morning

OPENERS
Fresh Fruit Plate (seasonal)

BREAKFAST SPECIAL
Rice Pudding

FROM GRANDMOTHER'S CELLAR
Apricots canned without sugar

BREAD BASKET
Fruit Bread & Apple Butter

RICE PUDDING

4 c. cooked rice or MILLET
1 c. raisins or chopped fruit
grated ORANGE RIND
slivered almonds or pecans
1 c. cashews
2 c. water
1/2 c. dates
1/8 tsp. salt
1 tsp. vanilla
2 tsp. maple flavoring

See page 41 for how to cook millet. Mix first four ingredients together. Blend the remaining ingredients and stir into cereal mixture. Bake at 350° for 40 min. until set.

FRUIT BREAD

4 c. dried fruit; raisins, dates, dried prunes, apricots, cherries,
*   pears, currants, use one or more*
2 c. chopped nuts, ie, walnuts
2 Tbs. grated ORANGE RIND
1 Tbs. anise, ground
1 Tbs. vanilla
2 c. fresh, peeled and cut apples
2 - 1# loaf bread dough recipes

In large bowl, cut up dried fruit. Add remaining ingredients. Mix together and add enough dough for two loaves; dough is at pan stage. With hands, knead and mix into dough all fruit mixture. Shape into 3-4 loaves. Place in oiled pans. Let rise and bake at 350° for 40-50 min.

APPLE BUTTER

2 apples
1/2 c. pitted dates
1/2 c. water

Wash, core and quarter apples. Cook apples with dates and water until apples are tender. Blend until smooth.

CANNED APRICOTS see page 209

29

Top of the Morning

OPENERS
Fruit Basket Selection

BREAKFAST SPECIAL
Sunny Boy Cereal (Plain or Left Over Pudding)
Favorite Milk

FROM GRANDMOTHER'S CELLAR
Canned Pears - without sugar
Strawberry Yogurt

BREAD BASKET
Bran or Blueberry Muffins
Grape Jam

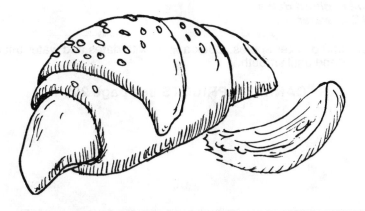

SUNNY BOY OR RED RIVER CEREAL

1 c. Sunny Boy, three grain cereal
3 c. water
3/4 tsp. salt

Bring water and salt to a boil in a covered saucepan. Stir in cereal. Cover, lightly boil for 30 minutes or until desired consistency.

LEFT OVER PUDDING

Pudding such as MILLET, RICE or BREAD PUDDING
Raisins or dates
Nuts
Flavorings
PEAR MILK

Put left over pudding in bowl, add raisins or dates to taste. Add chopped nuts and flavoring such as vanilla, maple flavoring, and orange rind to liking. Add enough thick PEAR MILK to make a sloppy consistency. Put in baking dish and bake at 350° until bubbly and golden brown on top. May add some fruit such as applesauce, or crushed pineapple to the above.

STRAWBERRY YOGURT

1 1/2 c. water
1/2 c. cashews
1/2 c. hot cooked rice or MILLET
1 c. frozen strawberries or other frozen fruit
1/4 c. soft dates
1/8 tsp. salt
1 tsp. lemon juice

See page 41 for how to cook millet. Whiz cashews and cereal in 1 c. water until smooth. Add remaining ingredients to blender. Chill and serve.

GRAPE JAM

4 c. grape juice
2 c. washed currants or raisins
1/4 c. Minute Tapioca

Mix together all ingredients. Let stand 30 minutes to soften fruit. Bring to boil over medium heat stirring constantly. Cook until tapioca is clear. Chill and serve. For a smoother jam blend smooth ingredients after cooking.

BLUEBERRY MUFFINS/BRAN MUFFINS see page 230

MILK see page 195

CANNED PEARS see page 209

31

Top of the Morning

OPENERS
Orange Sections or Fresh Apricots

BREAKFAST SPECIAL
Cornmeal, (Cooked Cornmeal, Baked Cornmeal Fingers)
Favorite Milk or Cream Topping

FROM GRANDMOTHER'S CELLAR
Canned or Stewed Apricots

BREAD BASKET
Apricot or Plum Balls

CORNMEAL

1 c. cornmeal
4 c. water
1/2 tsp. salt
1/2 tsp. maple flavor, optional

Slowly add cornmeal to boiling salted water. Cover and lightly boil 60 minutes. Add flavoring.

BAKED CORNMEAL FINGERS

Put warm cornmeal mush in a glass loaf pan. Chill in refrigerator. Unmold out of dish and cut into fingers. Roll in coconut. Put on greased cookie sheet and bake at 350° until golden brown. Can serve with maple syrup.

CREAM TOPPING

1 c. cooked rice or MILLET, hot
1/3 c. cashews
1 tsp. vanilla
1/4 c. chopped dates or 3 Tbs. honey
1/4 tsp. salt
1-1 1/2 c. water or MILK

Blend until creamy adding just enough water or milk to blend smooth. Chill.

PLUM OR APRICOT BALLS

Fresh plums or apricots
Dates
Favorite bread dough

Pit fresh plums or apricots and stuff with a date. Roll out dough 1/4 inch thick. Cut into rectangles about size of recipe card, depending on size of fruit. Wrap around stuffed fruit. Let rise on greased cookie sheet. Bake at 350° for 1/2 hour or more. May roll wrapped fruit in coconut before baking.

CANNED APRICOTS see page 209

MILKS see page 195

CREAM TOPPING see page 196

33

Top of the Morning

OPENERS
Green or Red Seedless Grapes

BREAKFAST SPECIAL
Crisp, (Fruit Crisp, Jan's Quick Fruit Crisp)
Pear Milk

FROM GRANDMOTHER'S CELLAR
Chunky Apple Sauce

BREAD BASKET
Peanut Butter & Bananas on Toast
Cherry Raspberry Jam on Banana Muffins

FRUIT CRISP #1

1 c. whole wheat flour
1 c. GRANOLA
3/4 c. almonds or walnuts, ground dry in blender
1/2 c. brown sugar or sucanat
1/2 tsp. salt
2 tsp. vanilla
water or PEAR MILK to moisten

Mix all ingredients and spread over about 6 c. sliced apples or any other fruit desired, in an 8 x 8 pan. Bake at 350° for 30 min., until fruit is soft. Granola may be ground in blender or left unground.

JAN'S QUICK FRUIT CRISP #2

6 c. canned fruit
scant almond flavoring
2 Tbs. minute tapioca

Into an 8 x 8 baking dish, put all ingredients. Mix well. Bake in oven at 350° until thickened, about 30 min. Remove from oven and put on crisp topping or ground granola. Return to oven and bake until top is browned, about another 30 min. If using granola, less time is needed.

CRISP TOPPING

1 1/2 c. oats
1/2 c. flour
1/2 c. coconut
1/3 c. brown sugar or sucanat
3 Tbs. PEAR MILK or water
1/2 tsp. salt
1 Tbs. vanilla
1/4 tsp. almond flavoring

Mix dry and wet ingredients separately, then combine together. Spread over fruit and bake as mentioned under fruit crisp. May need to increase baking time to 40-45 min. to lightly brown the topping.

BANANA MUFFINS see page 231

PEAR MILK see page 195

CHERRY RASPBERRY JAM see page 200

APPLESAUCE see page 209

Top of the Morning

OPENERS
Polished Red & Yellow Apples

BREAKFAST SPECIAL
Fruity Breakfast Pudding or Bread Pudding
Favorite Milk

FROM GRANDMOTHER'S CELLAR
Chunky Apple Sauce

BREAD BASKET
Jan's Wheat Germ Muffins

FRUITY BREAKFAST PUDDING

5 1/2 c. whole wheat bread crumbs
2 c. canned fruit
1/2 c. orange juice
1/8 tsp. almond extract
1 1/2 tsp. vanilla
1 c. raisins
3 large bananas

Make crumbs in blender. Blend canned fruit, 2 bananas, juice, 1/3 c. raisins and flavorings. Layer in greased 8 x 8 pan using: 1/3 crumbs, 1/2 blended liquid, 1/2 sliced banana, 1/3 c. raisins. Repeat, ending with bread crumbs. Bake at 325° for 40 minutes.

BREAD PUDDING

15 slices whole wheat bread, cubed
3 c. MILK
3/4 tsp. salt
1 1/2 c. raisins
1 tsp. vanilla
1 Tbs. grated ORANGE RIND
3 Tbs. honey, optional
1 or more banana
6 apples, peeled, chopped, optional

Blend bananas smooth in a small amount of water or MILK. Mix together all but bread cubes; fold these in last. Bake in a greased 8 x 8. If using apples bake in a 9x13 pan, at 350° for 45-60 minutes.

JAN'S WHEAT GERM MUFFINS see page 231

MILKS see page 195

APPLESAUCE see page 209

Top of the Morning

OPENERS
Oranges
Grapes, Fresh or Frozen

BREAKFAST SPECIAL
Cracked Wheat Cereal
Millet Sauce

FROM GRANDMOTHER'S CELLAR
Spring Rhubarb

BREAD BASKET
Breakfast Bread

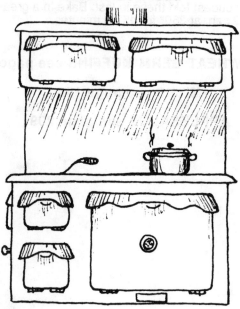

CRACKED WHEAT CEREAL

1/2 c. cracked wheat
2 c. water
8 dates, chopped
2 Tbs. sesame seeds, optional
2-3 Tbs. coconut
1/2 tsp. salt

Dextrinize or toast cracked wheat by stirring constantly in dry pan over low heat for several minutes or until lightly browned. Add remaining ingredients. Cover and bring to a light boil 20-30 minutes. Delicious sprinkled with chopped nut.

MILLET SAUCE

4 c. cooked MILLET, hot
2 c. pineapple juice
1/2 banana
1 Tbs. vanilla
1/3 c. honey, or more

See page 41 for how to cook MILLET. Do not pack MILLET when measuring. Mix together all ingredients. Blend smooth about 1/3 of the ingredients at a time. If the MILLET is hot, it will blend more smoothly. Serve warm or chill. Chilling will make it thicker.

SPRING RHUBARB

4 c. rhubarb, cut in 1 inch lengths
3/4 c. grape juice concentrate #1
1 c. apple juice concentrate
1/2 c. dates
1/2 c. apple juice concentrate #2

Bring to a boil equal amounts of apple juice concentrate and dates. Remove from heat and let dates soften. Blend smooth. Cook rhubarb with grape and apple juice #1 until tender. Stir in apple-date blend and cook 3 minutes. Bring to boil dates with 1/2 c. apple juice concentrate #2. Mashed strawberries may be added in season. This is a delicious rhubarb. The acid of the rhubarb overwhelms the date and juices so that it tastes only like rhubarb.
Note: Make several cups of the date/apple juice mixture ahead and freeze for use in sweetening fresh strawberries and other fruits.

BREAKFAST BREAD See Page 229

Top of the Morning

OPENERS
Fruit Basket of Oranges & Bananas
Fresh Cherries (while in season)

BREAKFAST SPECIAL
Millet (Plain, Millet Pudding, June's Millet Pudding)
Almond Milk

FROM GRANDMOTHER'S CELLAR
Cherries

BREAD BASKET
Coconut Raisin Buns
Peanut Butter
Dried Fruit Jam & Pineapple Prune Jam

MILLET

1 c. millet
4 c. water
1 tsp. salt

Bring water and salt to boil in a covered saucepan. Add millet. Cover. Lightly boil 1-2 hours. Do not stir while cooking.

MILLET PUDDING

4 c. cooked rice or MILLET
1 c. raisins or chopped fruit
2 tsp. grated ORANGE RIND or 1/2 tsp. dried orange peel
1/4 - 1/2 c. slivered almonds or pecans
1 c. cashews
2 c. water
1/2 c. dates
1/8 tsp. salt
1 tsp. vanilla
2 tsp. maple flavoring

See recipe above for how to cook millet. Mix together first four ingredients. Blend the remaining and pour over the cereal mixture. Bake in a greased dish at 350° for 40 minutes.

JUNE'S MILLET PUDDING

2 c. hot cooked MILLET
2 c. crushed pineapple or pineapple juice
1 banana, or 1 more cup of crushed pineapple
2 Tbs. Emes unflavored gelatin
2 tsp. vanilla
1/2 tsp. salt
2 Tbs. honey
2 c. ground granola
3 Tbs. flour
1/2 tsp. salt
2-3 Tbs. water

See recipe above for how to cook millet. Stir together first 7 ingredients. Blend smooth half of the mixture. Place in saucepan. Blend remaining mixture and add to pan. Bring to a light boil, stirring constantly, for a couple minutes. Then combine last 4 ingredients. Pat crust into a greased 8 x 12 pan. Bake at 350° for 30 minutes. Pour on pudding. Cool. Top with thickened blueberries or strawberries. Chill.

COCONUT BUNS see page 223. May add raisins to buns.

ALMOND MILK see page 195

DRIED FRUIT JAM/PINEAPPLE PRUNE JAM see page 201

THIS SPACE FOR YOUR NOTES & RECIPES

_____

_____

_____

_____

_____

_____

_____

_____

_____

_____

_____

_____

_____

_____

_____

_____

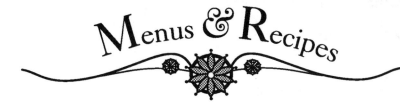

Menus & Recipes

Catchie Casseroles

CASSEROLES AND LOAVES

Introduction to the Protein Myth.

The Body's Protein Needs:

In sickness and in health one of the most important functions of our body is to rid itself of poisons constantly building up from the break down of food being digested. There are four ways the body has to get rid of these poisons: the lungs, the skin, the bowels, and the kidneys. At each of these exit stations the body uses water as the doorman. Even the lungs use water to rid the body of the gaseous waste carbon dioxide. You can tell that it is so by breathing on your glasses or mirror and you will see the drops of water. What does water and the body's need for it have to do with protein?

In the breakdown of protein the body produces urea, which is moved out of the blood by the kidneys. The more protein consumed the greater the need the body has for water to remove the urea produced as a result. Dr. Nathan Smith, professor of Athletic Medicine at the University of Washington in Seattle, likes to talk school athletes out of their protein habits. Energy can be more efficiently handled when it comes from complex carbohydrates like whole grains than from protein sources found in products of animal origin.

A number of years ago in Haiti thousands of children were suffering from a protein deficiency disease called Kwashiorkor. After being weaned, the babies were given starchy diets poor in protein and the mortality rate for children under four years of age was 50%. To meet the crisis they initiated an instruction program of three handfuls of grain to one handful of beans. As a result the protein deficiency was halted and eradicated from the island. Thanks to the understanding of medical science, a crisis was halted and lives were saved. But now we are faced by another dangerous problem of too much protein.

The fear of not having enough protein has led us to the opposite problem of too much protein. Even the false idea is presented that we need a certain kind of protein that can be obtained only from animal sources and that vegetable proteins are incomplete. There are populations around the world that eat 4% of their total calories as protein and these proteins are plant proteins.

Science indicates that the 100-plus grams a day protein intake of the average non-vegetarian American puts a tax on the liver and kidneys, triggers a loss of calcium from the bones, and also leaves behind a toxic residue which before being eliminated often damages the body and thus makes it more susceptible to a variety of diseases, including cancer and arthritis.

The question of how much protein the body needs varies from person to person, but the recommendation from the National Research Counsel is 46 grams for the ladies and 56 grams or 2 ounces for the men. These figures have been inflated by 30-50% because of allowing a margin of safety.

Adequate protein is easily available from a vegetarian diet. Here is a list of a few foods and the amount of protein they contain:

1 cup pinto beans - 15 grams of protein
1 baked potato - 5 grams
1 cup asparagus - 5 grams
2 slices of bread - 6 grams
1 cup broccoli - 6 grams
1 cup of green peas - 8 grams

Catchie Casseroles

CASSEROLE OF THE DAY
Millet Barley Loaf

POTATO (OR SUBSTITUTE)
Rice Potatoes
Mary's Gravy

VEGETABLE ACCOMPANIMENT
Corn on the Cob
Beets-Hawaiian Style

SALAD
Lettuce Salad

BREAD BASKET
Whole Wheat Toast

DESSERT
Carrot Pie or Tarts

MILLET BARLEY LOAF

1 c. cooked MILLET
1 c. cooked pearled barley
1/2 c. cashews, ground dry in blender
1/2 c. oats
1/2 c. water
1 Tbs. onion powder
2 Tbs. peanut butter
1/2 tsp. celery seed
1/4 tsp. thyme
1/8 tsp. cumin powder
salt to taste

See page 41 for how to cook millet. Mix well all ingredients. Put into oiled loaf pan and bake at 350° for 50 min. Let set. Slice. Serve with CASHEW GRAVY.

RICE POTATOES

Cook potatoes until thoroughly done but not mushy. Put through ricer. A nice change. Serve immediately for they cool quickly.

BEETS - HAWAIIAN STYLE

2 c. beets, cooked and cut
2/3 c. water
1 tsp. honey
1/4 tsp. salt
1 tsp. cornstarch
1 Tbs. water
2 Tbs. lemon juice
1 c. pineapple chunks

Combine first four ingredients and bring to boil. Dissolve cornstarch into the 1 Tbs. water. Add to beets. Continue to lightly boil 1 minute. Remove from heat and add lemon juice and pineapple. Serve hot or cold.

CARROT PIE/TARTS see page 262

MARY'S BROWN GRAVY see page 208

Catchie Casseroles

CASSEROLE OF THE DAY
Bread Dressing

POTATO (OR SUBSTITUTE)
Baked Potatoes
Soy Cream Cheese

VEGETABLE ACCOMPANIMENT
Fall Garden Medley

SALAD
Butter Crunch Lettuce
Tomato Slices
Tofu Mayonnaise

BREAD BASKET
Hot Steamed Buns

DESSERT
Carob Pie

BREAD DRESSING

6 c. cubed bread
1 1/2 tsp. sage
1 Tbs. CHICKEN STYLE SEASONING
  or 1/4 tsp. salt, 1/2 tsp. basil, 1/2 tsp. marjoram
2 Tbs. nutritional yeast, optional
1 c. almonds
2 c. water
1 tsp. salt
1 tsp. CHICKEN STYLE SEASONING or 1/8 tsp. salt
1 c. chopped celery
1 c. chopped onion

Mix first four ingredients together in bowl. Cube bread. Blend smooth next seven ingredients. Saute celery and onion. Add blended items to the vegetables. Stir in bread crumbs. Bake in oiled 8 x 8 pan at 350° for 50 minutes.

FALL GARDEN MEDLEY

1 onion, sliced and separated into rings
1 green pepper, sliced into strips
1 5-6 inch cabbage, shredded
2-3 c. canned tomatoes, chopped, with juice
1 6-oz. can pitted black olives, sliced
1/2 c. toasted sesame seeds
Garlic powder or granulated garlic to taste
TOFU SOUR CREAM

Place vegetables in layers in large pan with lid. Sprinkle sesame seeds over the top. Simmer until tender. Toss and serve with TOFU SOUR CREAM. Serve warm or chill and serve.

CAROB PIE FILLING

3 c. water & 1/2 c. cashews or 4 c. Tofu Milk
1 tsp. vanilla
1/4 tsp. salt
1 c. water
15 dates (add one at a time) or 1/2 c. sucanat or brown sugar
1/3 c. cornstarch or arrowroot powder
3 Tbs. carob powder
1 Tbs. Cafe Lib or Postum

Blend first four ingredients and continue to blend while adding the remaining ingredients. Bring to boil, stirring constantly till thick. Slice 1or 2 bananas in baked pie crust and pour filling over them. Chill.

SOY CREAM CHEESE see page 207

TOFU MAYONNAISE see page 202

49

Catchie Casseroles

CASSEROLE OF THE DAY
Zucchini Casserole

SALAD
Tomato, Cucumber, Olive Tray
Tropical Island Delight or Seasonal Fruit Salad
Pear Cream

BREAD BASKET
Hot Crusty Buns
Corn Butter
Garlic Butter

DESSERT
Banana Nut Cookies or Hawaiian Treats

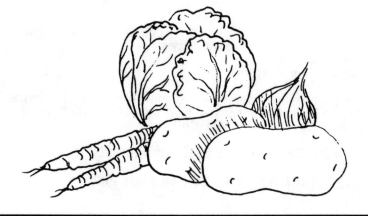

ZUCCHINI CASSEROLE

1 chopped onion
1 chopped green pepper
1 small, cubed zucchini
1 1/2 c. cooked corn
salt to taste
tomato sauce or TOMATO SOUP
cheese, of your choice

Saute first three ingredients. Add corn and salt. Pour into casserole and cover with tomato sauce or soup. Top with favorite cheese. Bake at 350° until bubbly.

TROPICAL ISLE DELIGHT SALAD

2 apples
2 oranges
2 bananas
1 c. crushed pineapple, drained
1 Tbs. honey, optional
3/4 c. dates, chopped
1 c. flaked coconut

Dice and toss first three ingredients. Add the remaining ingredients. Refrigerate two hours before serving. Garnish with slivered almonds. Serve with whole wheat rolls.

PEAR CREAM

1 c. cashews or blanched almonds
1/4 tsp. salt
1 tsp. vanilla
1-2 Tbs. honey
4 c. canned pears

Place first four ingredients into blender. Drain pears. Add juice to blender and blend smooth. Slowly add pears. Chill and serve.

HAWAIIAN TREATS

1 c. coconut
2 c. almond meal
2 c. ground dried pineapple

Place almonds in blender a few at a time to make a meal. Finely blend coconut. Grind pineapple in food grinder. Form into balls and roll in additional dried coconut. Makes 16 balls.

CORN BUTTER/GARLIC BUTTER see page 198

FRUIT SALAD see page 244

BANANA NUT COOKIES see page 250

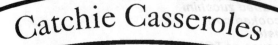

Catchie Casseroles

CASSEROLE OF THE DAY
Tofu Roast

VEGETABLE ACCOMPANIMENT
Tilly's Potatoes
Mary's Brown Gravy

SALAD
Lettuce Salad

BREAD BASKET
Sprouted Wheat Buns

DESSERT
Halvah Carob Balls

TOFU ROAST

2 lbs. tofu
1/4 c. chopped onion
1/2 c. chopped celery
2 Tbs. oil or water
1/2 c. MAYONNAISE
1/4 c. soy sauce
3/4 tsp. salt or less
2 c. bread cubes
1/8 tsp. garlic powder
1/8 tsp. sage

Drain and mash tofu. Saute onion and celery in water and/or oil. (More water will be necessary if not using oil while sauteing.) Mix all ingredients and place in greased loaf pan. Bake at 350° for 40 minutes.

TILLY'S POTATOES

12 cold, cooked potatoes grated on a large grater
1 small, finely grated onion
1/2 c. cashews
3/4 c. water
Salt to taste

Grate potatoes in a large grater. Finely chop onions. Blend smooth remaining ingredients. Mix all together well. Put in oiled casserole. Sprinkle with paprika. Cover and bake in oven at 350° for 45 minutes.

HALVAH CAROB BALLS

1 c. sesame seeds
1 c. almonds
1 c. sunflower seeds
1/2 c. honey

Grind first three ingredients 1 c. at a time in blender. Mix in honey. Form into balls. Dip in melted carob chips. Chill.

MARY'S BROWN GRAVY see page 208

SPROUTED WHEAT BUNS see page 221
Make buns from this bread recipe.

Catchie Casseroles

CASSEROLE OF THE DAY
Gluten Pinwheels

POTATO (OR SUBSTITUTE)
Scalloped Potatoes

VEGETABLE ACCOMPANIMENT
Parsnips & Carrots

SALAD
Cabbage Salad

BREAD BASKET
Dinner Rolls

DESSERT
Lemon Pie
Ice Cream

GLUTEN PINWHEELS

1 recipe pie crust
Hot mashed potatoes
GLUTEN STEAKS, ground

Make pie crust and roll in rectangular shape. Spread with hot mashed potatoes. Then spread gluten steaks. Roll up as a jelly roll and cut 1 1/2 inch thick. Place on greased cookie sheets cut side up. Bake at 350° until crust in brown, about 30 minutes. Serve with gravy.

SCALLOPED POTATOES

6 c. precooked potatoes, sliced
1 medium size onion
1 c. almonds, blanched
4 c. water
1 tsp. salt
1/4 c. flour

Precook potatoes. Cool and slice. Chop onion and saute slightly. Place in baking dish in layers. Blend smooth almonds, salt and flour with 1 1/2 c. water. Add remaining water. Bring to boil. Pour over potatoes. Top with PIMENTO CHEESE and bake at 350° until set, about 30 minutes.

CABBAGE SALAD

Chopped cabbage
1 c. shredded carrot
1 c. unsweetened crushed pineapple
1/2 c. nuts
Salt to taste
MAYONNAISE, of your choice

Mix well. Serve.

LEMON PIE FILLING

3 c. pineapple juice
1/4 tsp. salt
1 c. cashews, optional
1/4 c. brown sugar or honey
1/4 c. cornstarch or arrowroot
1 tsp. lemon rind
2 Tbs. lemon juice
1 Tbs. honey

Blend smooth first five ingredients. If using nuts blend smooth with 1 c. of juice before adding rest of ingredients. Bring to a light boil, stirring until thick. Remove from heat and add remaining ingredients. Put in baked pie shell and chill.

VANILLA ICE CREAM see page 271

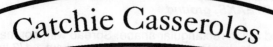

Catchie Casseroles

CASSEROLE OF THE DAY
Tamale Pie #1 or #2

VEGETABLE ACCOMPANIMENT
Pickled Beets

SALAD
Italian Salad

BREAD BASKET
Sprouted Wheat Buns

DESSERT
Lemon Pie
Coconut Cream

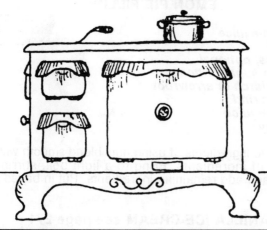

TAMALE PIE #1

1 6-oz. can olives, sliced or chopped
1 c. whole kernel corn, blended slightly
3 c. stewed tomatoes
2/3 c. cornmeal
3/4 tsp. cumin powder
3/4 tsp. oregano
1 small onion, chopped
1 garlic clove, minced
1/2 tsp. garlic powder
1/4 tsp. salt

Place olives in fry pan with 1 Tbs. water and simmer 2-3 minutes. Add and continue to saute onion and garlic, may need more water. Place corn and tomato sauce in same pan and stir well. Cook over low heat for 5 minutes. Add all the seasonings. Stir in the cornmeal and cook over low heat for 10 minutes and place in covered casserole dish. Bake at 325° for 30-40 minutes. Don't let get too dry.

TAMALE PIE #2

1 c. cornmeal
4 c. water
1/2-1 tsp. salt
3 c. cooked pinto beans, drained
1 onion, chopped
2 tomatoes, chopped, fresh or canned
1/2 green pepper, chopped
1 c. whole kernel corn
1 tsp. cumin
1 tsp. oregano
2 tsp. basil
1 minced clove garlic
1/2 tsp. salt

Cook cornmeal and water and salt on low for 15 minutes. Oil an 8 x 8 baking pan. Spread 1/2 cornmeal in bottom. Make mixture of remaining ingredients and spread over cornmeal. Spread remaining cornmeal over top. Bake at 350°, covered, for 1 hour. Garnish with shredded lettuce for each serving.

ITALIAN (MACARONI) SALAD see page 240

LEMON PIE FILLING see page 261

COCONUT CREAM see page 196

PICKLED BEETS see page 211

SPROUTED WHEAT BUNS see page 221
Make buns from this bread recipe.

Catchie Casseroles

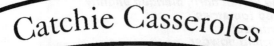

CASSEROLE OF THE DAY
Cashew Rice Loaf
Onion Gravy
Cranberry Sauce

POTATO (OR SUBSTITUTE)
Baked Squash

VEGETABLE ACCOMPANIMENT
Asparagus/Melty Cheese

SALAD
Carrot Coconut Salad

BREAD BASKET
Cornmeal Buns

DESSERT
Carob Fudge

CASHEW RICE LOAF

1 c. cooked brown rice
1 c. cashews, ground dry in blender
1 large onion, chopped and sauteed
2 slices whole grain bread, ground or blended
1/3 c. milk, nut or soy
1 Tbs. soy sauce
1/2 tsp. salt or to taste
1 Tbs. dried parsley
1/4 tsp. celery salt

Mix and place in well oiled baking pan. May bake in mold.Bake at 350° for 40 minutes.

ONION GRAVY

1 c. finely chopped onion
1 c. finely chopped celery
1/2 c. almonds or other nuts
1 c. water
1/3 c. white flour
2 tsp. CHICKEN STYLE SEASONING
1 tsp. salt
2 c. water

Saute onion and celery in saucepan. Blend almonds and water. Add remaining ingredients. Blend well and add to celery and onions. While stirring, lightly boil until thickened. If too thick, add more water.

CARROT SALAD see page 241

CORNMEAL BUNS see page 225

CAROB FUDGE #1 see page 252

CAROB FUDGE #2 see page 253

CRANBERRY SAUCE see page 212

MELTY CHEESE see page 206

Catchie Casseroles

CASSEROLE OF THE DAY
One Dish Meal

SALAD
Gisele's Greek Salad

BREAD BASKET
Bread Sticks

DESSERT
Carob Chip Cookies

ONE DISH MEAL

2 Tbs. water
1/2 c. chopped onion
1/2 c. chopped celery
1/4 c. chopped green peppers
1/2 c. chopped cooked carrots
1/4 c. cooked peas, optional
1 c. cooked garbanzo beans
3 c. cooked brown rice
1/4 c. chopped parsley
1 1/2 tsp. CHICKEN STYLE SEASONING or 1/8 tsp. salt and 1/2
   tsp. basil
1/8 tsp. oregano
1/2-1 tsp. salt

Saute onion and celery in water, add more if needed. Mix all ingredients together and bake in covered casserole dish at 350° for 30-40 minutes.

Variation: Add 1/2 c. chopped mushrooms.

GISELE'S GREEK SALAD

1 large onion
1 green pepper
1-2 tomatoes
1 cucumber
1/2 head cauliflower
1/3-1/2 head lettuce, optional
12 olives
GREEK SALAD DRESSING

Chop ingredients. Rub a large wooden salad bowl with garlic. Add all ingredients and toss. Add the following dressing.

GREEK SALAD DRESSING

1/4 c. water
1 Tbs. olive oil, optional
1/3 c. lemon juice
2 Tbs. honey
Vegie salt

Blend well. Add to salad. Let set 30-60 min. Serve with PARMESAN CHEESE.

BREAD STICKS see page 223

CAROB CHIP COOKIES #1 see page 247

61

Catchie Casseroles

CASSEROLE OF THE DAY
Lentil Loaf

POTATO (OR SUBSTITUTE)
Chips with Tomato Ketchup

VEGETABLE ACCOMPANIMENT
Broccoli or Fresh or Creamed Corn

SALAD
Carrot & Celery Sticks
Black Olives

BREAD BASKET
Clover Leaf Buns

DESSERT
Polynesian Bars

LENTIL LOAF

1 c. nuts, ground dry in blender
2 c. cooked lentils
1/2 c. cooked rice
1/2 c. bread crumbs
1 c. canned tomatoes, drained
1 tsp. salt
1/4 tsp. sage
2 Tbs. yeast flakes, optional
2 tsp. CHICKEN STYLE SEASONING or 1/4 tsp. salt and 1/2 tsp.
*   basil*
1 medium onion, chopped
1 c. celery, chopped
6 oz. can tomato paste

Cook 3/4 c. dry lentils in 2 c. of water until done, 45-60 minutes. Mix all ingredients together. Bake in oiled casserole for 60 minutes at 350°

POTATO CHIPS

Cut up cooked potatoes to desired thickness. Grease cookie sheetsand spread out on one layer. Salt if desired and put in preheated oven at 400°. Bake until crispy brown. Turn and bake, if necessary, on other side.

POLYNESIAN BARS

Filling:
2 c. chopped dates
4 c. crushed pineapple
3/4 c. water
1 tsp. vanilla

Crumb mixture:
3/4 c. whole wheat flour
3/4 c. unbleached white flour
3/4 tsp. salt
1 1/2 c. quick oats
1 c. nut butter
1/2 c. coconut
1/2 c. chopped nuts

Mix together and cook filling ingredients until dates are soft, about 5 minutes. Mix together ingredients from crumb mixture. Press half of mixture into a 9 x 13 oiled pan. Spread filling over crumb mixture. Put remaining crumbs on top and pat down well. Bake at 350° for 30-40 minutes. Cool and cut in squares.

KETCHUP see page 212

63

Catchie Casseroles

CASSEROLE OF THE DAY
Irish Stew
served with a wholesome variety of garden vegetables
Baked in Mary's Gravy

SALAD
Tossed Green Salad
French Dressing

BREAD BASKET
Cornmeal Buns

DESSERT
Kathy's Tofu Cheesecake
Thickened Pineapple & Raisins

Garlic

IRISH STEW

Peas
Potatoes
Carrots
Turnips
Celery
Cauliflower
GLUTEN STEAKS, cut and fried
MARY'S GRAVY

Cut the vegetables into big bite size pieces. Cook first three together. Steam celery and cauliflower. Chop onion and saute. Arrange all vegetables in deep roasting pan. Add fresh or frozen peas. Add gluten. Pour gravy over and sprinkle with paprika. Cover and bake 40 minutes at 350°.

MARY'S BROWN GRAVY

1/2 c. almonds or cashews
1 c. water
2 c. water
1/4 c. whole wheat flour
1/8 tsp. garlic salt
1 tsp. salt
1 tsp. CHICKEN STYLE SEASONING or Beef Style Seasoning
1 tsp. soy sauce
1 tsp. Marmite or 1 tsp. Vegex or 1 1/2 T. soy sauce

Blend almonds and 1 c. water until smooth. Add remaining ingredients. Blend well. Bring to boil, stirring constantly. If too thick add more water.

FRENCH DRESSING see page 204

KATHY'S TOFU CHEESECAKE see page 268

Catchie Casseroles

CASSEROLE OF THE DAY
Gluten Steaks

POTATO (OR SUBSTITUTE)
Mashed Potatoes
Cashew Gravy

VEGETABLE ACCOMPANIMENT
Peas & Carrots

SALAD
Chinese Cabbage Salad
Thousand Island Dressing

BREAD BASKET
June's Buns

DESSERT
Carob Chip Clusters

BETTY'S GLUTEN STEAKS

4 c. 100% instant gluten flour
1/2 c. whole wheat flour
1/2 c. unbleached white flour
1/2 c. minute tapioca
1/4 c. yeast flakes
3 Tbs. CHICKEN STYLE SEASONING
3 Tbs. garlic powder
1/4 c. soy sauce
3 1/4 c. cold water

Mix dry ingredients well and add all at once to the liquid ingredients. Mix fast and knead. Shape into two rolls. Put in plastic bags. Freeze. When ready to cook, partly thaw, slice thin and boil in broth. To have partially frozen makes cutting easier but if only needing chunks, freezing is not necessary.

BROTH

12 c. water
1 onion, chopped
1 garlic clove, chopped
2/3 c. soy sauce
1/4 c. yeast flakes
3 Tbs. CHICKEN STYLE SEASONING
2 Tbs. oil, optional

Combine ingredients for broth and bring to boil. Add steaks while it continues to boil. Simmer for 1 1/2 hour.
Ways to serve gluten:
1) Saute lots of onions and make gravy with leftover broth. Dip gluten slices in the following breading meal, then fry on a non-stick griddle.
  1 part cornmeal
  1 part flour
  1 part yeast flakes
Put in casserole. Top with onions, pour gravy over, heat and serve.
2) Bread steak slices with yeast flakes and fry on non-stick griddle or fry pan. Serve.
3) Burger: Grind gluten steaks, put in fry pan or griddle. Sprinkle with yeast flakes and brown, turning several times. Ready to use for Stroganoff, Sloppy Joes, etc.

CASHEW GRAVY see page 208

CABBAGE SALAD see page 240

THOUSAND ISLAND DRESSING see page 204

CAROB CLUSTERS see page 253

THIS SPACE FOR YOUR NOTES & RECIPES

_____

_____

_____

_____

_____

_____

_____

_____

_____

_____

_____

_____

_____

_____

_____

Menus & Recipes

Pleasing

Patties

THIS SPACE FOR YOUR NOTES & RECIPES

_____

_____

_____

_____

_____

_____

_____

_____

_____

_____

_____

_____

_____

_____

_____

BURGERS AND PATTIES

Every culture is known for its favorite food. What would England be without its fish and chips, Italy without its pizza, Mexico without its tortillas and beans, or North America without its burgers and fries. Gone are the days of bragging up Mom's good home cooking. Family favorites can only be bought at the local fast food outlets. Unfortunately this change is affecting the health of every family member from the youngest to the eldest.

We eat far differently from our ancestors. We consume 40% of our calories in the form of fats. The burger and fries combination adds up to a heavy fat meal. Because of the changes in our methods of agriculture and meat production, the product being sold is different from what it was at the turn of the century. Cattle are not the same range fed muscular lot they once were. Today cattle are confined in feed lots, grain is fed to fatten them, and their flesh becomes marbled with fat. As a result, even after trimming off all the visible fat, at least 40% of what is left is fat. What about the side order of fries? The humble, nutritious potato, after it has been fried, changes from a healthy 140 calories for an 8 ounce potato to 375 calories.

So what is all this fat up to in the body? The different sources of fat create different problems as far reaching as heart and blood vessel diseases like hardening of the arteries. Vegetable fats, such as vegetable oils used in cooking, have been associated with aging and the foundation for cancer and diabetes. Over and above all these diseases there is still the heavy problem of obesity and weight control. In this section you will find good news. You can have burgers and fries without the worries of fat, and you will hear the praises of Mom's cooking for many years to come.

Pleasing Patties

SPECIAL PATTY OF THE DAY
Fish Sticks

VEGETABLE
Stewed Tomatoes, Onions, Zucchini

SALAD
**Cucumber Salad
Lo Cal Mustard
Relish
Tarter Sauce**

BREAD
Garlic Bread

DESSERT
**Brad's Frozen Blueberry Delight
Granola Bars**

FISH STICKS

1 c. quick or rolled oats
2 c. water
2 Tbs. CHICKEN STYLE SEASONING
1 c. chopped onions
1 c. cracker or bread crumbs
3/4 c. FLAXSEED JELL
3 c. TOFU COTTAGE CHEESE

Mix together all ingredients. Spread evenly on oiled cookie sheet. Bake at 275 for 50-60 min. Let stand several hours to thicken. Slice. Ready to use or freeze. When ready to use dip in a crumb mixture of corn flake crumbs and onion powder or other breading mix. Fry slowly until golden brown. Serve with TARTAR SAUCE.

TARTAR SAUCE

2 Tbs. PICKLE RELISH
1/2 c. TOFU MAYONNAISE
salt to taste

Mix well and chill to combine flavors.

CUCUMBER SALAD

1 c. fresh lemon juice
1/2 c. honey
1/2 tsp. salt, or more
4 c. sliced cucumbers
1/2 c. thinly sliced sweet onions
2 Tbs. finely minced parsley, fresh

Mix together first three ingredients. Pour over salad items and toss. Refrigerate for a few hours stirring occasionally.

GRANOLA BARS

1 c. peanut butter
1/2 c. honey
1/2 c. coconut
1 Tbs. vanilla
3 Tbs. flour
1/4 tsp. salt
4 c. granola

Warm and soften in saucepan first four ingredients. Mix together remaining ingredients. Combine all together. Press into oiled pan and cut. Bake at 350° until brown. Approximately 10-20 minutes.

LO-CAL MUSTARD see page 211
BRAD'S FROZEN BLUEBERRY DELIGHT see page 272
GARLIC BUTTER see page 198

Pleasing Patties

SPECIAL PATTY OF THE DAY
Big Macs

POTATO
French Fries
Ketchup

VEGETABLE
Marinated Vegie Salad

SALAD
Green Tossed Salad

BREAD
Dinner Rolls

DESSERT
Cocoa Peanut Butter Balls

BIG MAC

1/2 c. cooked garbanzo beans
1/2 c. water
1 c. uncooked rolled oats
1/2 c. finely chopped walnuts
1 onion, minced
1 Tbs. CHICKEN STYLE SEASONING or 1/4 tsp. salt and 1/2
  tsp. basil
3/4 tsp. salt
1 Tbs. soy sauce
1/2 tsp. sage
2 Tbs. yeast flakes, optional

Blend garbanzo beans and water until smooth. Add remaining ingredients. Mix well. Let stand 1/2 hour. Shape into patties. Brown on both sides in a non-stick skillet. Or bake in oven at 350° on an oiled cookie sheet for 30 min. Flip and continue to bake 10-20 min. until firm and browned.

POTATO CHIPS/FRENCH FRIES

Cut up cooked potatoes to desired thickness. Grease cookie sheets and spread out on one layer. Salt if desired and put in preheated oven at 400°. Bake until crispy brown. Turn and bake if necessary on other side.

Variation: May slice 10 raw potatoes. Toss with 1 Tbs. olive oil and 1 tsp. salt. Place in greased cookie sheet. Bake 35 minutes at 400°. Flip potatoes when lightly browned, after about 20 minutes.

MARINATED VEGI SALAD

1/2 c. lemon juice
1/2 c. honey
1-2 tsp. seasoning salt
1 15 oz. can whole kernel corn, drained
1 15 oz. can French style green beans, drained
1 17 oz. can peas, drained
1 c. chopped celery
1 c. chopped raw carrots
1 medium onion, diced
1 small jar pimento for color, optional

Combine first three ingredients. Mix remaining items. Pour dressing over top, stir and refrigerate. Serve chilled.

COCO-PEANUT BALLS see page 249

KETCHUP see page 212

Pleasing Patties

SPECIAL PATTY OF THE DAY
Soya Oat Patties

VEGETABLE
Baked Squash

SALAD
Greek Pasta Salad

BREAD
Grilled Cheese Sandwiches/Buns

DESSERT
Cashew Date Banana Tarts

SOY OAT PATTIES

1 c. soaked soy beans
1/2 c. water, approximately
2 Tbs. yeast flakes, optional
2/3 c. chopped onion
1/2 c. chopped celery
1/4 tsp. garlic powder
1 Tbs. dry or 2 Tbs. fresh parsley
1/2 tsp. Italian seasoning
1/2 - 3/4 tsp. salt
3/4 c. oats

Combine all ingredients except rolled oats, onion and celery in blender. Place in bowl. Add remaining ingredients; let stand 10 minutes to absorb moisture. Shape into patties. Brown both sides in a non-stick skillet. Serve with tomato sauce. Or bake on cookie sheet at 350° for 30 minutes. Flip and continue to bake 10-20 minutes, until firm.

GRILLED CHEESE SANDWICHES #1

1 c. water
3/4 c. cashews
1 Tbs. sesame seeds
1 1/4 tsp. salt
1/4 tsp. ground dill seed
1/8 tsp. garlic powder
3 Tbs. yeast flakes
1/2 c. or 1-4 oz. jar canned pimento
1 Tbs. arrowroot powder or cornstarch
1/3 c. lemon juice

Blend smooth all ingredients. Cook, stirring constantly, until thick. Spread whole wheat bread with cheese filling, add a slice of tomato if desired. Spread CORN BUTTER on outside of bread and toast in non-stick skillet on both sides.

Variation: In a small bowl mix 2 Tbs. cornstarch, 1 c. water, 1/4 tsp. salt. Dip the outsides of the sandwiches in this mixture and place on greased cookie sheet. Bake in oven about 10-15 minutes on each side. Delicious!

GRILLED CHEESE SANDWICHES #2
using JACK CHEESE see page 205

GREEK PASTA SALAD see page 240

CASHEW DATE BANANA TARTS see page 262

Pleasing Patties

SPECIAL PATTY OF THE DAY
Millet Patties

POTATO SUBSTITUTE
Debbie's Special Cabbage Salad

VEGETABLE
Green Bean-Beet Salad

BREAD
Buns
Soy Cream Cheese

DESSERT
Pumpkin Pie
Vanilla Ice Cream #1

MILLET PATTIES

1 1/2 c. cooked MILLET
1 c. mashed potatoes
1/2 c. rolled oats
1/2 c. nuts, ground dry in blender
1 c. onion, chopped
1/2 c. water
1 tsp. salt
2 Tbs. CHICKEN STYLE SEASONING
3-4 Tbs. yeast flakes

See page 41 to cook millet. Mix all ingredients together. Shape into patties. Brown on both sides in a non-stick skillet. Or bake on oiled cookie sheet at 350° for 30 minutes. Flip and continue to bake 10-20 minutes, until firm. Serve as a sandwich in a bun. Or place in baking dish, pour gravy or tomato sauce over and bake until heated.

DEBBIE'S SPECIAL CABBAGE SALAD

1/2 c. peanuts or sunflower seeds
1 small cabbage or 1/2 medium head
4 sliced green onions
1 package uncooked Ramen Noodles, without seasoning
*   packet, or Chow Mein Noodles*
MAYONNAISE or DRESSING, of choice

Shred cabbage and add the onions. Mix in any kind of dressing and refrigerate. Crumble the dry, uncooked Ramen or chow mein noodles, combine with peanuts and set aside. Just before serving, mix all ingredients together.

GREEN BEAN-BEET SALAD

3 c. cooked, drained green beans
3 c. cooked, coarsely shredded beets
1/3 c. honey
1/2 c. lemon juice
1 tsp. salt

Stir together honey, lemon juice and salt. May add other seasonings if desired such as onion powder, parsley flakes, garlic powder. Mix all ingredients and let stand, stirring occasionally to marinate well.

SOY CREAM CHEESE see page 207

PUMPKIN PIE see page 262

VANILLA ICE CREAM #1 see page 271

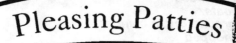

Pleasing Patties

SPECIAL PATTY OF THE DAY
Shamburgers

POTATO
Hash Browns
Ketchup

VEGETABLE
Broccoli
Golden Carrots

SALAD PLATE
Fresh Vegies on Romaine Lettuce
Tofu Mayonnaise with Fresh Dill

BREAD
Rye Bread

DESSERT
Minute Tapioca

SHAMBURGERS

2 1/2 c. oats
1 c. raw sunflower seeds, ground dry in blender
1 1/8 c. hot water, hot tofu or soy milk
1 Tbs. gluten flour
1 Tbs. onion powder

Mix and let stand 30 minutes. Divide burger dough into small balls. Brown slightly.

Broth:
4 c. water
1/3 c. soy sauce
2 Tbs. parsley flakes
1 Tbs. CHICKEN STYLE SEASONING or 1/2 tsp. salt

Bring to boil in large kettle. Drop balls into boiling broth. Cover and lightly boil for 1 hour and 15 minutes.

HASH BROWNS

Dice cold precooked potatoes. Using a non-stick skillet, lightly grease and put in cut up potatoes. May add a little CHICKEN STYLE SEASONING and garlic salt if you wish. Fry until crispy.

GOLDEN CARROTS

4 c. sliced raw carrots
1/2 tsp. salt
1 1/2 c. water, or the amount needed to cook carrots
2 1/2 c. pineapple chunks
2 Tbs. cornstarch
1/4 tsp. salt

Cook carrots until tender in 1 1/2 c. water with the 1/2 tsp. salt. Drain, reserving 1 c. of the water in which the carrots were cooked. Drain pineapple chunks, reserving juice. Stir cornstarch into the 2 liquids. In a small pot cook cornstarch and salt mixture until it thickens and bubbles. Mix carrots and pineapple chunks in a serving dish and pour sauce over. Serve.

KETCHUP see page 212

TOFU MAYONNAISE see page 202

MINUTE TAPIOCA see page 265

RYE BREAD see page 222

Pleasing Patties

SPECIAL PATTY OF THE DAY
Walnut Burgers

FIXINGS
Potato Salad

VEGIES & SALAD
Tray of Lettuce & Tomatoes
Dill Pickles
Marinated Onions

BREAD
Grilled Burger Buns with Jack Cheese

DESSERT
5 Minute Carob Cake
Carob Ice Cream

WALNUT BURGERS

2 c. bread crumbs
2 c. cooked brown rice
1 c. chopped walnuts
1 c. thick cashew milk, blend smooth 1/3 c. nuts and 3/4 c.
    water
1/2 tsp. salt
1/4 c. soy sauce
1 onion, chopped fine
2 ribs celery, chopped fine
1 Tbs. chopped parsley
2 Tbs. gluten flour or 1/4 c. whole grain flour

Combine all ingredients and form into patties and brown on both sides in non-stick skillet. Or bake at 350° on oiled cookie sheet 35 minutes. Flip, continue to bake 10-15 minutes. Or may place in oiled casserole and bake at 350° for 45 minutes as a loaf. Tip: To form patties place wax paper in bottom of wide mouth jar ring and put patty mixture on wax paper and press down to fill out rim. Turn onto skillet and peel off wax paper.

GRILLED CHEESE SANDWICHES #1

1 c. water
3/4 c. cashews
1 Tbs. sesame seeds
1 1/4 tsp. salt
1/4 tsp. ground dill seed
1/8 tsp. garlic powder
3 Tbs. yeast flakes
1/2 c. pimento or 1-4 oz. jar canned pimento
1 Tbs. arrowroot powder or cornstarch
1/3 c. lemon juice

Blend smooth all ingredients. Cook, stirring constantly until thick. Spread whole wheat bread with cheese filling and a slice of tomato if desired. Spread CORN BUTTER on outside of bread and toast in non-stick skillet on both sides.
Variation: In a small bowl mix 2 Tbs. cornstarch, 1 c. water, 1/4 tsp. salt. Dip the outsides of the sandwiches in this mixture and place on greased cookie sheet. Bake in oven at 350° about 10-15 minutes on each side. Delicious!

GRILLED CHEESE SANDWICHES #2 see page 205

MARINATED ONION SLICES see page 237

POTATO SALAD see page 239

DILL PICKLES see page 210

5 MINUTE CAROB CAKE see page 256

CAROB ICE CREAM see page 271

Pleasing Patties

SPECIAL PATTY OF THE DAY
Millet Meat Balls

POTATO SUBSTITUTE
Hot Rice Salad

VEGETABLE
Peas

BREAD
Buns
Garlic Butter
Lo Cal Mustard
Ketchup

DESSERT
Blueberry Pie
Pear Grape Sherbet

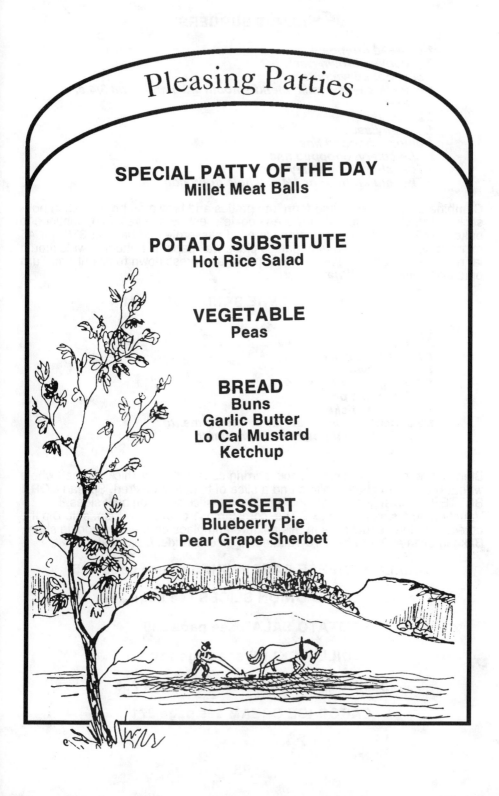

MILLET MEATBALLS

4 c. cooked MILLET
1 tsp. salt
2 Tbs. paprika, optional
1 c. finely ground bread crumbs
2 c. pecans or walnuts, chopped fine
1 c. sunflower seeds, ground dry in blender
2 Tbs. CHICKEN STYLE SEASONING or 1/2 tsp. salt
4 tsp. onion powder
1 tsp. oregano
1 Tbs. nutritional yeast flakes, optional

See page 41 for how to cook millet. Mix above ingredients and form into balls. Place on oiled cookie sheet. Bake at 350° for 30-40 minutes until brown. Turn once, while baking. May also bake as patties.

HOT RICE SALAD

2 c. brown rice
1/2 tsp. salt
5 c. water
1 large tomato, chopped
1 cucumber, chopped
1 c. green onion, chopped
1 small green pepper, chopped
1 avocado, diced
Soy sauce to taste

Bring water and salt to a boil in covered saucepan. Add rice, cover. Lightly boil 1 hour. Do not stir while cooking. Remove from heat. Add remaining ingredients and toss. Garnish with toasted sunflower seeds. Serve warm.

GARLIC BUTTER see page 198

LO-CAL MUSTARD see page 211

KETCHUP see page 212

BLUEBERRY PIE see page 261

PEAR GRAPE SHERBET see page 272

Pleasing Patties

SPECIAL PATTY OF THE DAY
Oat Burgers

POTATO
Scalloped Potatoes

VEGETABLE
Creamed Brussel Sprouts

SALADS
Spinach Salad
Garnished with Toasted Sunflower Seeds

BREAD
Whole Wheat Bread
Corn Butter

OAT BURGERS

2 1/2 c. boiling water
2 Tbs. marmite or 1/4 c. soy sauce
2 tsp. garlic salt
1 Tbs. CHICKEN STYLE SEASONING or 1/2 tsp. salt
1 c. walnuts or pecans, ground
3 c. quick oats
1/4 tsp. celery salt
1/2 c. onion, chopped fine
1/2 c. celery, chopped fine

Pour boiling water over oats and seasonings. Let absorb 10 minutes. Add remaining ingredients. Brown on both sides in a non-stick skillet. Or oil cookie sheet and bake patties at 350° for 30 min. flip continue to bake 10-15 min.

SCALLOPED POTATOES

6 c. precooked potatoes, sliced
1 medium size onion
1 c. almonds, blanched
4 c. water
1 tsp. salt
1/4 c. flour

Precook potatoes. Cool and slice. Chop onion and saute slightly. Place in baking dish in layers. Blend smooth almonds, salt and flour with 1 1/2 c. water. Add remaining water. Bring to boil. Pour over potatoes. Top with PIMENTO CHEESE and bake at 350° until set, about 30 minutes.

VERNA'S OATMEAL SQUARES

4 c. oats
1 c. coconut
1 1/2 c. whole wheat flour
1 c. brown sugar
1 tsp. salt
2 Tbs. flaxseed, optional
1 c. raisins or dates
1 c. chopped nuts
1 c. nut butter
1 c. carob chips, optional

Mix together all ingredients. May need a little water to get the right consistency for bars. Pat into oiled pan approximately 1/2 inch thick. Score. Bake for 35 minutes at 350°.

CORN BUTTER see page 198

CREAMED BRUSSEL SPROUTS see page 235
See creamed green beans

WHOLE WHEAT BREAD see page 220

THIS SPACE FOR YOUR NOTES & RECIPES

_____

_____

_____

_____

_____

_____

_____

_____

_____

_____

_____

_____

_____

_____

_____

Menus & Recipes

Pass
the
Pasta

THIS SPACE FOR YOUR NOTES & RECIPES

_____

_____

_____

_____

_____

_____

_____

_____

_____

_____

_____

_____

_____

_____

_____

_____

PASTA, CHEESE AND MOLDS

In a paper by the Health Protection Branch of Canada there was an interesting article called, "Mold, More Than Meets the Eye".

At sometime most of us will see or have seen moldy food. Our natural inclination is to scrape mold away so that the food is not wasted. Before doing so, we should first consider the following facts: Some molds produce toxins called mycotoxins (stemming from the Greek word meaning mushroom which is also a type of fungus). Unfortunately, it is not possible to tell which molds produce mycotoxins and which molds are harmless simply by looking at them. Consequently, removing visible surface mold growth from a food and eating the food could be dangerous. If the mold has produced mycotoxins they may have seeped under and around the mold growth. Some of these mold toxins are highly toxic even in small amounts and in animal tests have been found to cause cancer. Some mycotoxins can survive for a long time in food. Some are not even destroyed by heat; so cooking won't help.

In 1960, 100,000 turkeys died in England due to mycotoxins in moldy peanut meal. Since that time awareness of the harmful effects of mold has prompted better storage and handling of all food stuffs. Not all molds are considered as dangerous to health as the naturally occurring molds found in food. But it is well to consider the following:

During the fermentation or curing of cheese a mixed group of microorganisms grow in the milk curd. Here is a summary of the objectionable features of hard or ripped cheese.
1) During the fermentation process amines, ammonia and irritating fatty acids are produced. The carbohydrate is converted to lactic acid. These are all waste products which cause irritation to nerves and gastrointestinal tract.
2) Migraine headaches can be caused by tyramine, one of the toxic amines produced in cheese.
3) Certain of the amines can interact with the nitrates present in the stomach to form nitrosamine, a cancer producing agent.
4) An intolerance to lactose, the chief carbohydrate of cheese and milk, is probably the most common food sensitivity in America. One favorite dish enjoyed by many is macaroni and cheese. Now you can have one of your favorite pasta dishes without the problems that come along with cheese.

Tip for Cooking Pasta:

All pasta should be added to a large amount of rapidly boiling water to ensure that the boiling is not disturbed and the pasta has room to cook. An approximate guideline is 4-5 parts water to one part pasta. For every 3 quarts of water add 1/2 tsp. salt. If the water stops boiling after the pasta is added bring the water back to a boil and cover tightly. Turn the heat off. Set the pan aside for 30 minutes. Don't peek. Drain, rinse and serve.

Pass the Pasta

MAIN COURSE
Spaghetti

VEGETABLE ACCOMPANIMENT
Broccoli/Cauliflower Spears

SALAD
Gisele's Greek Salad
Black Olives

BREAD
Garlic Bread

DESSERT
Kathy's Tofu Cheesecake

SPAGHETTI TOMATO SAUCE

1 1/2 c. zucchini, optional
1/2 green pepper, diced
1 med. onion, diced
28 oz. canned tomatoes or 3 1/2 c. tomato juice
6 oz. tomato paste
2 Tbs. sweetening, optional
1 tsp. basil
1 tsp. salt
1 tsp. paprika
1 bay leaf
1/2 tsp. cumin, optional
1/4 tsp. dry minced garlic or 1 tsp. fresh garlic
1 can black olives, sliced, optional

Saute first three ingredients. Add remaining ingredients and simmer over low-med. heat until sauce is thick. Remove bay leaf. If using juice, stir in 1/3 c. unbleached white flour into 1 c. of juice. Bring remaining juice and other ingredients to a boil. Add juice with flour. Bring to light boil, stirring. Cook until thickened. Cook noodles. Serve separate and let family put sauce on noodles or combine noodles and sauce and bake in oven.

GISELE'S GREEK SALAD

1 large onion
1 green pepper
1-2 tomatoes
1 cucumber
1/2 head cauliflower
1/3-1/2 head lettuce, optional
12 olives
GREEK SALAD DRESSING

Chop ingredients. Rub a large wooden salad bowl with garlic. Add all ingredients and toss. Add the following dressing.

GREEK SALAD DRESSING

1/4 c. water
1 Tbs. olive oil, optional
1/3 c. lemon juice
2 Tbs. honey
Vegie salt to taste

Blend well. Add to salad. Let set 30-60 min. Serve with PARMESAN CHEESE.

GARLIC BUTTER see page 198

KATHY'S TOFU CHEESECAKE see page 268

Pass the Pasta

MAIN COURSE
Tofu Manicotti

VEGETABLE ACCOMPANIMENT
Peas

SALAD
Cucumber Salad

BREAD
Clover Leaf Buns

DESSERT
Apple Pie
Pear Cream

TOFU MANICOTTI

1 lb. tofu, drained, mashed
1-10 oz. package frozen spinach or 1 bag fresh spinach
2/3 c. cashews
2/3 c. water
1-2 garlic cloves, minced
1 Tbs. lemon juice
1/2 tsp. salt
1 Tbs. yeast flakes, optional
2 tsp. basil, optional
1 tsp. oregano, optional
*TOMATO SAUCE, may use recipe on page 93 or 173 or your
    favorite*

Cook spinach and garlic together. Chop until fine and drain. Blend smooth cashews and water. Stir together all ingredients. Fill cooked shells with stuffing. Place in casserole. Top with tomato sauce. Bake at 350° for 30 minutes, or until heated.

CUCUMBER SALAD

1 c. fresh lemon juice
1/2 c. honey
1/2 tsp. salt
4 c. sliced cucumbers
1/2 c. thinly sliced sweet onions
2 Tbs. finely minced parsley

Mix together first three ingredients. Pour over salad items and toss. Refrigerate for a few hours stirring occasionally.

CLOVER LEAF BUNS

Use basic bread dough recipe. Oil muffin tins. Roll each clover leaf bun into three balls the size of cherries. Place into muffin tins. Let rise. Bake at 350° for 25-30 minutes.

CRUMBLE TOP APPLE PIE see page 263

PEAR CREAM see page 196

Pass the Pasta

MAIN COURSE
Lasagna

VEGETABLE ACCOMPANIMENT
Baby Carrots/Peas

SALAD
Boc Choy & Carrot Salad

DESSERT
Carmen's Tropical Cheese Cake

LASAGNA

*TOMATO SAUCE, may use recipe on page 93 or 173 or your
    favorite*
PIMENTO CHEESE, MELTY CHEESE or JACK CHEESE
Cooked lasagna noodles
Tofu or ground GLUTEN STEAKS

Put layer of sauce in bottom of pan, noodles, sauce, tofu or browned ground gluten, cheese, noodles, sauce, cheese. Bake at 350° for 1 hour.

Note: Can use uncooked noodles. Layer as above, but tightly cover pan with foil. Bake at 350° for 60 minutes. Uncover and bake for 15 minutes to brown top.

CARROT SALAD

2 carrots, shredded fine
1/2 c. celery, or boc choy, chopped
1/4 c. walnuts, chopped or 1/4 c. coconut
1/4 c. crushed pineapple
3 Tbs. raisins
1/4 c. MAYONNAISE, choose one from index

Mix well. Serve.

CARMEN'S TROPICAL CHEESE CAKE

Crust:
1 1/2 c. granola
2 Tbs. honey
1 Tbs. water

Cheese filling:
2 c. tofu, drained and crumbled
1 Tbs. lemon juice
1 Tbs. vanilla
1 Tbs. maple flavoring
1-20 oz. can crushed pineapple
2 Tbs. cornstarch or arrowroot powder
1 banana
1/2 c. honey

Filling: Mix filling ingredients together. Blend smooth half of the ingredients. Repeat blending process. Pour the blended ingredients on top of the crust recipe. Bake at 350° for 25-30 minutes until edges are lightly browned and center is firm. Chill.

Crust: Blend granola until fine in blender. Mix crust ingredients together. Press into oiled 8 x 8 baking dish. Bake. Chill. Top with favorite thickened fruit before serving.

Pass the Pasta

MAIN COURSE
Macaroni and Cheese

VEGETABLE ACCOMPANIMENT
Homesteader Peas

SALAD/SALAD PLATE
Thanksgiving Salad on Lettuce Leaf
Ripe Green Olives
Tomatoes
Side Dish of Parmesan Cheese

BREAD
Dinner rolls

DESSERT
Upside Down Cake
"Pear" Orange Sherbet

MACARONI AND CHEESE

1 1/4 c. water
1/2 c. red pepper or canned pimento
3/4 c. cashews
3 Tbs. yeast flakes
1 1/4 tsp. garlic salt
1 tsp. onion powder
1/2 c. lemon juice
4 c. cooked soy macaroni or other favorite macaroni

Blend all ingredients except macaroni. Bring sauce to boil, stirring until thickened. Pour sauce over cooked macaroni. Mix and put in baking dish. Sprinkle with seasoned bread crumbs. Bake 350° for approximately 30-40 minutes.

THANKSGIVING SALAD

2 c. diced, tart red apples
1 c. chopped nuts
1 c. diced celery
1/2 c. raisins or diced pitted dates
3/4 c. TOFU MAYONNAISE
1-2 Tbs. LO CAL MUSTARD
6 lettuce cups

Mix together all ingredients except lettuce. Serve on lettuce cup.

UPSIDE DOWN CAKE

Filling:
2 c. thickened blueberries
2 Tbs. GRATED ORANGE RIND or 1 tsp. dried peel
2/3 c. walnut halves
5-6 shredded apples
Batter:
1 3/4 c. white flour
1/4 c. whole wheat flour
1 Tbs. health baking powder
1/2 tsp. salt
1/4 c. peanut butter
1/4 c. white or brown sugar, date sugar or honey
1 1/4 c. cold water
1/2 tsp. maple flavoring and 1/2 tsp. vanilla

Oil an 8 x 12 baking pan. Mix first three items of filling. Pour into baking pan. Next add shredded apples. Bake at 400° for about 15-20 minutes to let apples partially cook. Mix first four ingredients of batter then cut in peanut butter. Add remaining ingredients and mix well. Spread this over apple mixture. Bake at 400° for 35-40 minutes.

PARMESAN CHEESE see page 205

PEAR ORANGE SHERBET see page 272

Pass the Pasta

MAIN COURSE
Tofu Shells

VEGETABLE ACCOMPANIMENT
Four Bean Salad

SALAD PLATE
Tomatoes, Cucumbers, Olives

BREAD
Sesame Buns

DESSERT
Strawberry Pie
Vanilla Ice Cream #2

TOFU SHELLS

4 c. partially cooked manicotti shells or stuffing shells
1 c. cashews or almonds
3 c. water
2 Tbs. white flour
2 tsp. CHICKEN STYLE SEASONING
1 Tbs. soy sauce
1 tsp. salt
1 c. chopped celery, sauteed
1 c. chopped onions, sauteed
1 lb. firm tofu
2 Tbs. CHICKEN STYLE SEASONING
vegetable salt to taste
2/3 c. crushed pineapple
1/3 c. chopped green peppers
1/3 c. baco bites or 1/2 c. ground GLUTEN STEAKS

Blend nuts with 1 c. water. When smooth, add remaining water and next four ingredients. Bring to a light boil. Add sauteed celery and onions. Stir until thickened. Mash tofu with next two ingredients. Then add last three. Fill cooked shells with tofu mixture. Pour sauce over. Bake at 350° for 40 minutes.

FOUR BEAN SALAD

2 c. kidney beans, cooked
2 c. garbanzo beans, cooked
2 c. green beans, cooked
2 c. wax beans, cooked
1/2 c. sliced olives
1 c. diced celery or more
2 small onions sliced in rings
1 lg. green pepper, cut in strips
2 Tbs. pimento, cut in strips
1/2 c. lemon juice
1/2 c. honey
salt to taste

Drain beans well, mix all except lemon juice, honey and salt. Whiz these in blender or shake well in jar, pour over all and allow to marinate in refrigerator for 6 hours or overnight.

SESAME SEED BUNS

Use basic bread recipe. Form into buns and dip in sesame seeds.

VANILLA ICE CREAM #2 see page 271

STRAWBERRY PIE see page 261

Pass the Pasta

MAIN COURSE
Burmese Kawk Sauce over Soy Noodles

VEGETABLE ACCOMPANIMENT
Green and Wax French Beans

SALAD
Deluxe Tossed Salad
Lemon/Honey/Dill Dressing

BREAD
Hot Dinner Rolls
Corn Butter

DESSERT
Fruit Salad Delight
Fruit Candy

Lemon

BERMESE KAWK SAUCE

1 large onion
4 cloves garlic
1 tsp. salt
8 c. coconut milk
2 Tbs. curry powder, see page 213
1/2 c. Baison flour (pea flour)
2 Tbs. CHICKEN STYLE SEASONING
Vegetarian Chicken chunks or Gluten pieces
Soy Noodles
Finely chopped green onions
Lemon juice, fresh if possible

Saute onions and garlic. Add curry powder and coconut milk and salt. Put in cubes of chicken or beef, or gluten chunks which ever you prefer, and simmer for 15 minutes, then add chicken style seasoning and thicken with Baison flour. Boil noodles separately and pour sauce over noodles in individual dishes Garnish with green onions and fresh lemon juice according to taste.

Coconut Milk: Blend smooth 1 cup coconut and 1 cup water. Add 3 more cups of water while blending. Strain. Repeat process with more coconut and water to make 8 cups of coconut milk.

FRUIT CANDY

2 c. seedless raisins
2 c. walnuts
2 c. chopped dates
pinch of salt

Mix and put through food grinder. Make into small balls and roll in coconut. Store in covered container in refrigerator.

FRUIT SALAD DELIGHT

1 c. + 1 heaping Tbs. of Emes flavored gelatin
1 1/2 c. boiling water
1 qt. peaches
1 large tin pineapple
1 small can of oranges

Dissolve gelatin in boiling water. Drain juice of the fruit into 4 c. measuring cup. Add enough cold water to juice to make total of 2 1/2 c. of liquid. Add to dissolved jello.Cool and pour over fruit and refrigerate.

CORN BUTTER, see page 198

THIS SPACE FOR YOUR NOTES & RECIPES

_____

_____

_____

_____

_____

_____

_____

_____

_____

_____

_____

_____

_____

_____

_____

_____

Menus & Recipes

Bean

Bonanza

THIS SPACE FOR YOUR NOTES & RECIPES

_____

_____

_____

_____

_____

_____

_____

_____

_____

_____

_____

_____

_____

_____

_____

_____

BEANS

Weight for weight, ordinary dry beans and lentils contain about the same percentage of protein as does fresh meat, or about twice as much protein as found in grains. The quality of protein in beans enhances the proteins found in grains as demonstrated by the following experiment: Upon adding only 5% of soy flour to 95% of wheat flour, the quanity and quality of protein is increased; and in experimental animals this combination gives twice the growth promoting value of wheat flour alone. Thus the protein found in peas supplements well that found in wheat. Other good combinations are whole wheat bread and peanuts or peanut butter, or whole wheat bread and beans.

These are good combinations for making a complete protein but don't be overly concerned about eating these combinations at the same meal. The body has a storage of amino acids from foods eaten. It makes the necessary protein from this amino acid storage. The important point is to get a variety of foods on a daily basis.

Flatulence-Intestinal gas

Sometimes when people make rather abrupt changes in their diet they encounter problems with flatulence (gas) formed in the intestinal tract. This is especially true for people who make major changes in diet, such as from the typical American high fat, high sugar, low fiber diet to the low fat, high complex carbohydrate, high fiber diet recommended in this book.

Following are some suggestions for people who are troubled by flatulence:

1. Beans, peas and bran may cause gas problems. Experiment with eating these foods in small amounts or eliminate them from the diet altogether and then re-introduce them gradually in small amounts.
2. Lightly cooked vegetables cause less gas formation than all raw vegetables.
3. Overeating can be a factor in flatulence. Chew food longer and learn to relax at mealtime.
4. Avoid swallowing air while eating. Chewing with the mouth open contributes to swallowing air.
5. Soak legumes 6 to 8 hours then discard soaking water. Add fresh water to cook the beans in.
6. Eliminate carbonated beverages.
7. Lactose (milk sugar) causes flatulence for some people.
8. Be patient. The choice to change the diet is worth the effort. The problem of flatulence will usually pass with time.

Approximate Cooking Time for Legumes

Item	Simmering on stove top in covered saucepan
Lentils	45-60 minutes
Navy Beans	2-3 hours
White Lima Beans	2-3 hours
Great White Northern Beans	2-3 hours
Green Split Peas	45-60 minutes
Green Whole Peas	3-4 hours
Yellow Split Peas	45-60 minutes
Black-eyed Peas	1-2 hours
Kidney Beans	2-3 hours
Chili Beans	2-3 hours
Pinto Beans	2-3 hours
Soy Beans	4-6 hours
Garbanzos	4-6 hours
Rice (brown, long or short grain)	1-2 hours

THIS SPACE FOR YOUR NOTES & RECIPES

_____

_____

_____

_____

_____

_____

_____

_____

_____

_____

_____

_____

_____

_____

_____

Bean Bonanza

IN THE BEAN POT
Chili
Served over Rice

SALAD OF THE DAY
County Garden Pea Salad

BREAD
Corn Tortillas

DESSERT
Orange Apricot Pudding

CHILI

2 c. dry kidney beans
3 1/2 c. water
2 c. chopped onion
1 c. chopped green pepper
1 c. chopped celery
2 1/2 c. tomatoes
6 oz. can tomato paste
2 tsp. salt
2 tsp. cumin
2 tsp. celery seed
1 tsp. paprika
1 garlic clove

Cover beans with 8 c. of water and soak for at least 8 hours. Drain. Cook beans until soft in the 3 1/2 c. of water either on the stove or in a pressure cooker. Add remaining ingredients and continue to cook 30 min. 2 c. ground gluten may be added.

CORN TORTILLAS

1 c. cornmeal
1 c. boiling water
2-2 1/2 c. whole wheat flour
salt

Pour the boiling water over the cornmeal. Let stand 5 minutes. Mix salt and flour. Add enough flour to the cornmeal mixture to make a kneadable soft dough. Knead 5 minutes. Let sit 5 minutes. Pinch off a piece of dough the size of a golf ball. Roll out on a floured board in the shape of a circle about 4 inches in diameter. Cook on an unoiled hot griddle or in a skillet, about 2 minutes on each side.

ORANGE APRICOT PUDDING see page 266

COUNTRY GARDEN PEA SALAD see page 241

Bean Bonanza

IN THE BEAN POT
Pottage - Chef's Choice:
Mazidra or Italian Lentils

SALAD OF THE DAY
Salad Plate if #2 is your choice

BREAD
Sesame Dinner Rolls

DESSERT
Crumble Top Apple Pie
Pear Maple Walnut Ice Cream

MAZIDRA

5 1/2 c. water
2 c. lentils
1 small onion, chopped
1 1/2 tsp. salt
1 Tbs. soy sauce
1 tsp. marjoram
1/8 tsp. thyme
1 bay leaf
2-3 c. cooked brown rice, hot
shredded lettuce
diced tomatoes
diced avocado
chopped olives
lemon juice, optional
garlic salt
tomato sauce

In a covered pan, lightly boil first eight ingredients for 45 minutes. Assemble on plate the following ingredients: Cooked brown rice, lentils, shredded lettuce, diced tomatoes, diced avocado, chopped olives, lemon juice, garlic salt and your favorite tomato sauce.

ITALIAN LENTILS

2 c. dry lentils, soaked overnight then drained
water
2 c. stewed tomatoes
1 chopped onion
2 garlic cloves, minced
3/4 tsp. salt
1/4 tsp. oregano
1/4 tsp. cumin
6 oz. can tomato paste, optional

Place soaked lentils in saucepan and add water to cover. Add remaining ingredients and lightly boil 45 min. When done, add 1 tsp. olive oil, as this brings out more flavor.
Serve over brown rice. Delicious made with fresh tomatoes pureed in blender instead of canned.

CRUMBLE TOP APPLE PIE see page 263

PEAR MAPLE WALNUT ICE CREAM see page 272

Bean Bonanza

IN THE BEAN POT
Garbanzo Goulash
Noodles

SALAD OF THE DAY
Waldorf Salad

BREAD
Pocket Bread

DESSERT
Verna's Oatmeal Squares or Puffed Wheat Bars
Brad's Frozen Blueberry Delight

GARBANZO GOULASH

4 c. canned tomatoes
4 c. cooked garbanzo beans
1 large onion, chopped
1 green pepper, chopped
1 clove garlic, minced
salt to taste
2 Tbs. yeast flakes
1-2 Tbs. CHICKEN STYLE SEASONING
4 c. cooked noodles, optional
1/3 c. tomato paste

Combine and bring to boil: tomatoes, onion and green pepper. Simmer 15 minutes. Add seasonings and simmer another 30 min. Then blend 2 c. of beans with just enough water to make a thick creamy consistency. Add to tomato mixture. Put rest of garbanzos in and bring to boil again. May add noodles. Heat and serve.

WALDORF SALAD

Apples, cubed
Walnuts, chopped
Raisins

Cream:
1 part cashews
2 parts water
honey and vanilla to taste
dash salt

Blend cream ingredients smooth. Add to salad.

BRAD'S BLUEBERRY FROZEN DELIGHT

1/4 c. almonds or cashews
2 c. water
1/4 c. raisins or soft dates
1/8 tsp. salt
1-4 frozen banana chunks, according to taste
Frozen blueberries

Blend smooth dried fruit, nuts and salt with 1 c. of water. Add remaining cup of water. Use half of this mixture to blend 1 of 2 bananas and enough blueberries to make desired thickness. Repeat with other half of nut mixture and more bananas and blueberries. Pretty if garnished with coconut.

POCKET BREAD see page 226

POPCORN OR PUFFED WHEAT BARS see page 251

VERNA'S OATMEAL SQUARES see page 252

Bean Bonanza

IN THE BEAN POT
Haystacks
Pinto Beans

SALAD OF THE DAY
Lazy Susan Tray of Chopped:
Lettuce, Cucumbers, Celery
Tomatoes, Cheese, Dill Pickles, Onion
Served with Tofu Mayonnaise
Fresh Dill

BREAD
Corn Chips
Jack Cheese or Melty Cheese

DESSERT
Tofu Cheese Cake with Thickened Blueberries

HAYSTACKS

1 c. pinto beans
2 1/2 c. water, add more as needed
2 cloves garlic, minced
1 Tbs. CHICKEN STYLE SEASONING or 3/4 tsp. salt, 1 tsp.
  basil
1/2 tsp. cumin, optional
salt to taste
1/3 c. chopped green pepper

Soak dry beans in 3 c. of water for 6 hours or longer. Drain. Cook beans in covered pan with 2 1/2 c. water, add more if needed. Cook until beans are soft, about 2 1/2 hours. Add remaining ingredients and continue to cook 30 minutes. Make double batch of CORN CHIPS. Cut up different vegetables, pickles. Make TOFU MAYONNAISE and serve with favorite CHEESE.
When serving:
Begin with corn chips. Serve beans on top. Then desired vegetables and pickles and etc. Top with mayonnaise and cheese.

CORN CRACKERS OR CHIPS

1 1/4 c. water
1 Tbs. coconut
1 1/2 Tbs. sesame seeds
1/4 c. cashews or coconut
1/4 c. oats or barley flakes
1 tsp. salt
1/2 c. water
3/4 c. cornmeal
3/4 c. oats or barley flakes
onion and garlic powder, optional

Blend first six ingredients well then add remaining ingredients and blend again. Pour small amount into greased muffin tins in middle. Tip from side to side to spread evenly, quite thin. Bake at 350° until golden brown, approximately 5-8 minutes. As batter sits in bowl, it gets thicker, add a little bit of water from time to time.

I always have an extra pan ready so I can keep an assembly line going to make it go faster. If you are having them the next day just reheat in a pan for a few minutes to crispen.

TOFU MAYONNAISE see page 202

MELTY CHEESE see page 206

JACK CHEESE see page 205

TOFU CHEESE CAKE see page 267

Bean Bonanza

IN THE BEAN POT
Sweet & Sour Casserole

SALAD OF THE DAY
Cabbage Salad
Green Bean Beet Salad

BREAD
Rye Bread
Corn Butter
Garlic Butter

DESSERT
Lemon Pie with Coconut Cream Topping

SWEET AND SOUR CASSEROLE

2 c. dry lima beans
2 Tbs. soy sauce
1 bay leaf
1 Tbs. olive oil
1/2 c. brown sugar
1 Tbs. cornstarch
1/2 c. water
6 tofu wieners, cut, optional
salt to taste
1/2 c. lemon juice

Wash beans, soak in 6 c. of water at least 6 hours. Drain. Cook beans in 5 c. of water until tender, about 2 1/2 - 3 hours, add more water if necessary. Add remaining ingredients to beans. Bake at 350° for 60 minutes.

LEMON PIE FILLING

3 c. pineapple juice
1/2 tsp. salt
1 c. cashews, optional
1/4 c. brown sugar
1/4 c. cornstarch or arrowroot
1 tsp. lemon rind
2 Tbs. lemon juice
1 Tbs. honey

Whiz first five ingredients in blender. If using cashews first blend them with 1 c. juice. When smooth then add remainder of first five ingredients. Stir and simmer over low heat until clear. When thick, remove from heat and add remaining ingredients. Put in baked pie shell and chill. Top with COCONUT CREAM.

COCONUT CREAM

2 c. water
2/3 c. coconut
1/4 c. cornstarch
2 Tbs. honey
1/4 tsp. salt

Blend coconut and water for 1 minute. Add remaining ingredients and blend. Stir over medium heat until thickened. Chill and serve. Great with LEMON PIE.

CABBAGE SALAD see page 240

GREEN BEAN-BEAT SALAD see page 242

CORN BUTTER see page 198

GARLIC BUTTER see page 198

RYE BREAD see page 222

Bean Bonanza

IN THE BEAN POT
**Sloppy Joe's served with a variety of choices:
Over Rice, on Grilled Buns or Toast, in Pocket Bread or
rolled up in Lefsa**

SALAD OF THE DAY
Cucumber Salad

DESSERT
**Fresh Apple Cake
Pear Ice Cream
Strawberries**

SLOPPY JOES

1 qt. canned tomatoes
2 c. FRENCHIES TOMATO SOUP
1/3 c. tomato paste
1 tsp. honey
1-2 chopped onions
1 chopped green pepper
1 c. chopped celery
2-2 1/2 c. ground browned GLUTEN STEAKS

Combine first four ingredients in saucepan. Saute onions, green pepper and celery. Stir together all ingredients. Simmer and serve over brown rice, as an openface sandwich on grilled buns or in pocket bread or rolled in Lefsa.

CUCUMBER SALAD

1 c. fresh lemon juice
1/2 c. honey
1/2 tsp. salt, or more
4 c. sliced cucumbers
1/2 c. thinly sliced sweet onions
2 Tbs. finely minced parsley, fresh

Mix together first three ingredients. Pour over salad items. Refrigerate for a few hours stirring occasionally.

PEAR ICE CREAM

1 c. cashews or blanched almonds
1 c. water or pear juice
1/4 tsp. salt
1 tsp. vanilla
1/3 c. honey
1 tsp. slippery elm powder, optional
1 qt. canned pears

Blend all but pears until creamy. Gradually add canned pears. Pour into flat dish. Cover. Freeze. Cut in strips and put through Champion Juicer, or blender or food processor. May need to let soften slightly in order to blend.

Bean Bonanza

IN THE BEAN POT
Baked Navy Beans:
Hawaiian or Cowboy
French Fries/Ketchup

SALAD OF THE DAY
Salad Plate of:
Buttercrunch Lettuce
Tomatoes
Olives
Relish

BREAD
Lefsa or
Whole Wheat Toast

DESSERT
Blachinda
Orange Ice Cream

BAKED NAVY BEANS

2 c. dry navy beans
3 Tbs. molasses
1 1/2 tsp. salt
4 c. tomato juice or blended canned tomatoes
1/2 c. tomato paste
1/2 c. unbleached wheat flour
1 Tbs. lemon juice
1 Tbs. honey
1/2 tsp. celery salt
1/2 tsp. garlic powder
1 lg. onion, sliced

Soak dry beans in 6 c. of water at least 6 hours. Drain. Cook in 6 c. water until soft, approximately 2 1/2 hours. Drain. Add remaining ingredients. Put in casserole dish and top with some sliced onion. Bake at 300° for at least 2 hours.

For Hawaiian Beans-add pineapple chunks.
For Cowboy Beans-add sliced Tofu Wieners. Purchase wieners in health food store.

POTATO CHIPS/FRENCH FRIES

Cut up cooked potatoes to desired thickness. Grease cookie sheets and spread out on one layer. Salt if desired and put in preheated oven at 400°. Bake until crispy brown. Turn and bake, if necessary, on other side.

KETCHUP

6 oz. can tomato paste
1 Tbs. honey
1 tsp. salt
3 Tbs. lemon juice
1/4 tsp. garlic powder
1/4 tsp. onion powder

Tomatoes, tomato juice or water enough to make the mixture blend. Whiz until smooth. Store in refrigerator.

BLACHINDA see page 260

ORANGE ICE CREAM see page 271

Bean Bonanza

IN THE BEAN POT
June's Beans, Beans, Beans
Hash Browns

SALAD OF THE DAY
Cucumber Salad

BREAD
Clover Leaf Buns

DESSERT
Boiled Raisin Cake
Carob Ice Cream

JUNE'S BEANS, BEANS, BEANS

1 c. white navy beans
1/2 c. pinto beans
1/2 c. kidney beans
1/2 c. baby lima beans
1 med. onion, chopped fine
1 tsp. salt
2 Tbs. molasses
1 Tbs. olive oil, optional

Soak beans together overnight in 2 qts. of water. Boil for 5 minutes and drain. Put onion in bottom of bean pot or casserole. Add other ingredients, cover with water and bake at 300° for 3-4 hours.

HASH BROWNS

Cut up cold precooked potatoes. Using a nonstick skillet, lightly grease and put in cut up potatoes. Can add a little CHICKEN STYLE SEASONING and garlic salt if you wish. Fry until crispy.

CUCUMBER SALAD

1 c. fresh lemon juice
1/2 c. honey
1/2 tsp. salt, or more
4 c. sliced cucumbers
1/2 c. thinly sliced sweet onions
2 Tbs. finely minced parsley

Mix first three ingredients. Pour over salad items. Refrigerate for a few hours stirring occasionally.

CLOVER LOAF BUNS

Use a basic bread dough recipe. Oil muffin tins. Roll dough into balls the size of cherries. Place three balls side by side into each muffin cup. Let rise 30 minutes. Bake at 350° for 25-30 minutes.

BROILED RAISIN CAKE see page 255

CAROB ICE CREAM see page 271

THIS SPACE FOR YOUR NOTES & RECIPES

_____

_____

_____

_____

_____

_____

_____

_____

_____

_____

_____

_____

_____

_____

_____

Menus & Recipes

Nice
with
Rice

THIS SPACE FOR YOUR NOTES & RECIPES

_____

_____

_____

_____

_____

_____

_____

_____

_____

_____

_____

_____

_____

_____

_____

_____

RICE

The history of the building of our Canadian Railway yields interesting details on the use of rice. Apparently the imported Oriental laborers lived largely on rice and vegetables. A candid picture handed down from those bygone days was the typical weekend celebration of the railroad workers. The local towns people were hard put by the hard working, beer drinking, rough and tumble laborers seeking diversion from the grueling work of primitive road building. On the other side of town were the pagan Oriental laborers harmlessly eating their rice and vegetables undisturbing even the most feeble citizens. Even today the idea prevails that to be big and strong takes a lot of muscle food that can be had only from the thick almost raw steaks. Dr. Stare of Harvard University has well observed that lumberjacks may demand plenty of red meat but that demand rests on habits and not on nutritional or medical basis. The Chinese coolie, although not large of stature, will draw a load of freight at the speed of a horee's trot for a distance of 30-40 miles at a time. His diet consists of rice, dates, vegetables and rarely a small portion of fish. The Hindu messengers who carry dispatches long distances day after day live principally on rice. In fact, in a test done by Swedish scientists on endurance, it was discovered that a diet high in fat and protein from meat sources gave a maximum work time of sixty minutes, whereas a diet high in grains, provided a maximum work time of 150 minutes. Actually endurance is the test of strength, and rice is a delicious way to add variety to the meat and potatoes habit.

Nice with Rice

MAIN COURSE
Cabbage Rolls

VEGETABLE ACCOMPANIMENT
Four Bean Salad

SALAD PLATE
Waffled Carrots, Celery, Radishes

BREAD
Rye Bread

DESSERT
Peanut Butter Cookies

CABBAGE ROLLS

1) Preboil large cabbage leaves for about one minute to make them tender. Drain them well. Use a knife to shave away part of the thick central ribs so the leaf will be easy to roll. Option: wash, core cabbage and place in plastic bag. Microwave until tender, taking off leaves as ready.

2) Put a handful of stuffing on the stem end of the leaf. Fold the leaf end and sides over the stuffing. Roll up the leaf from the stem end to make a neat parcel.

3) Holding the packages carefully to prevent them from unwrapping, put them in a casserole with the free ends of the leaves underneath. Pack them closely so that they cannot unroll. Use favorite tomato sauce or FRENCHIES TOMATO SOUP to cover rolls. Cover casserole and bake at 350° for about 1 1/2 hours.

STUFFING

1 large chopped onion
1 c. finely chopped celery
2/3 c. nuts
2 1/2 c. water
1 Tbs. CHICKEN STYLE SEASONING or 1/2 tsp. salt, 1 tsp.
  basil, 1/2 tsp. oregano
1 tsp. salt
4 c. cooked rice
1/2 c. cornmeal, uncooked
1/2 c. baco bits, optional or 1 c. ground GLUTEN, optional

Saute first two ingredients. Blend nuts smooth with 1 c. of water. Add remaining water, seasoning, and salt. Add onions and celery and stir until bubbling. Add to rice and cornmeal. Mix. This is prepared stuffing.

FRENCHIES TOMATO SOUP

8 c. V-8 juice or seasoned tomato juice
2 Tbs. olive oil
1/3 c. + 1 Tbs. flour
1 tsp. salt
2 Tbs. honey

Mix flour with 1 c. of juice. Bring to boil remaining ingredients. Add juice with flour, stirring until thickened. Put in 2 c. cooked rice for tomato rice soup.

FOUR BEAN SALAD see page 241

RYE BREAD see page 222

PEANUT BUTTER COOKIES see page 248

131

Nice with Rice

MAIN COURSE
Spinach Bake

VEGETABLE ACCOMPANIMENT
Corn on the Cob
Pickled Beets

SALAD
Carrot Coconut Salad

BREAD
Open Faced Grilled Cheese Sandwiches

DESSERT
Cashew Crumbles

SPINACH BAKE

10 oz. pkg. frozen spinach
3 c. cooked rice
2-3 c. JACK CHEESE
1/2 c. minute tapioca
2/3 c. mayonnaise
1/4 c. chopped onion

When making cheese leave out the Emes gelatin. Mix all ingredients. Bake in oiled casserole at 350° for 60 minutes.

GRILLED CHEESE SANDWICHES, OPEN FACE

1/2 c. water
1/4 c. Emes unflavored gelatin
3/4 c. boiling water
1 c. cashews
1/4 c. yeast flakes
1 1/2 tsp. salt
1 tsp. onion powder
1/4 tsp. garlic powder
1/4 c. lemon juice
3 Tbs. finely grated carrot or pimento or red pepper to color

Soak gelatin in the 1/2 c. water in blender, while assembling remaining ingredients. Pour boiling water over soaked gelatin and whiz briefly to dissolve. Add cashews and blend smooth. Add remaining ingredients. Continue to blend smooth. Pour into greased container, cool slightly. Cover and refrigerate overnight before using. Slice on bread and grill in oven.

CARROT SALAD

2 carrots, shredded fine
1/2 c. celery, chopped
1/4 c. walnuts chopped or 1/4 c. coconut
1/4 c. crushed pineapple
3 Tbs. raisins
1/4 c. MAYONNAISE

Mix well. Serve.

PICKLED BEETS see page 211

MELTY CHEESE see page 206

CASHEW CRUMBLES see page 249

Nice with Rice
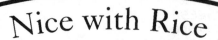

MAIN COURSE
Chow Mein's Chinese Food:
Baked Rice
Sweet & Sour Sauce

VEGETABLE ACCOMPANIMENT
Stir Fry Vegetables

SALAD
Chinese Cabbage Salad
Olives

BREAD
Brown Bread
Garlic Butter

DESSERT
Sesame Fingers

BAKED RICE

Put desired amount of uncooked rice in bottom of a baking dish. Then put in double the amount of hot water. For example: 2 c. rice to 4 c. water. Stir in desired amount of salt. Cover tightly and put in oven at 350° for 60 minutes. A nice way to serve plain rice.

SWEET AND SOUR SAUCE

3 c. pineapple juice
6 oz. can tomato paste
3 Tbs. soy sauce, optional
1 Tbs. honey
1 Tbs. lemon juice
2 Tbs. arrowroot powder
1/2 c. cold water
salt to taste

Bring first five ingredients to boil. Add arrowroot powder mixed in cold water. Stir and cook until thickened. Serve vegetables, sweet and sour sauce and rice.

STIR FRY VEGETABLES

2 c. sliced celery
1 sliced green pepper
2 c. onions, cut in eighths
2 c. sliced carrots
peas or edible-pod peas

Steam vegetables in pineapple juice, soy sauce, CHICKEN STYLE SEASONING or salt and water. Add seasonings of choice such as onion salt, basil, CHICKEN STYLE SEASONING, or garlic powder.

Variations: Use other vegetables such as sliced broccoli or cauliflower, bean sprouts or bok choy. May add crumbled tofu to vegetables or sliced almonds.

DEBBIE'S SPECIAL CABBAGE SALAD

1/2 c. peanuts or sunflower seeds
1 sm. cabbage or 1/2 med. head
4 sliced green onions
1 pkg. uncooked Ramen Noodles without seasoning packet or
* chow mein noodles*
DRESSING or MAYONNAISE, of choice

Shred cabbage and add the onions. Mix in any kind of dressing and refrigerate. Crumble the dry, uncooked noodles, combine with peanuts and set aside. Just before serving, mix all ingredients together.

GARLIC BUTTER see page 198

SESAME FINGERS see page 252

135

Nice with Rice

MAIN COURSE
Marilyn's Hawaiian Rice

VEGETABLE ACCOMPANIMENT
Peas/Corn on the Cob

SALAD/SALAD PLATE
Tiny Tim Tomatoes
Black Olives
Cucumber Salad

BREAD
Sesame Bread Sticks

DESSERT
Molasses Chews, Hawaiian Treats or Date Balls

HAWAIIAN RICE

1 c. chopped celery
1 c. chopped onion
1 c. green or red pepper
1 c. cashews or almonds
1/4 c. flour
4 c. water
2 c. pineapple juice
1-2 Tbs. soy sauce
garlic salt
2 Tbs. honey
1/4 c. lemon juice
1 tsp. celery seed
20 oz. can crushed pineapple

Saute first three ingredients. Blend cashews, flour, and 1 1/2 c. water until smooth. Then add remaining water. Pour into saucepan. Add pineapple juice and stir until boiling. Add remaining ingredients. Stir in vegetables. Serve over rice. Sprinkle with slivered almonds.

DATE BALLS

3 c. chopped dates
1 tsp. vanilla
1 c. water
2 c. cereal flakes
1 c. chopped nuts

Simmer first three ingredients stirring constantly until soft. Cool and add remaining ingredients. Drop with teaspoon into flaked coconut and roll into balls. Store in refrigerator. Makes 75 balls.

HAWAIIAN TREATS

1 c. coconut
2 c. almond meal
2 c. ground dried pineapple

Place almonds in blender a few at a time to make a meal. Blend coconut until fine. Grind pineapple in food grinder. Form into a ball and roll in additional dried coconut. Makes 16 balls.

HONEY MOLASSES CHEWS see page 249

CUCUMBER SALAD see page 243

BREAD STICKS see page 223

Nice with Rice

MAIN COURSE
Best Stroganoff

VEGETABLE ACCOMPANIMENT
Tender Homesteader Peas

SALAD PLATE
Dill Pickles/Avocadoes
Tiny Tim Tomatoes

BREAD
Hot Clover Leaf Buns

DESSERT
Blueberry Pie
Vanilla Ice Cream #1

STROGANOFF

2 onions, chopped fine
1 c. chopped green pepper, optional
1 c. chopped celery
1 c. almonds or cashews
1/2 c. flour
4 c. water
1/2 tsp. garlic salt
1 tsp. celery salt
2 Tbs. CHICKEN STYLE SEASONING
1 tsp. salt
2-3 Tbs. soy sauce or Maggi
1/4 recipe GLUTEN STEAKS
1/2 c. TOFU MAYONNAISE

Saute first three ingredients. Blend smooth almonds, and flour with 1 1/2 c. water. Add remaining seasonings and water. Bring to boil in saucepan, stirring constantly. Add vegetables and gluten. Just before serving add mayonnaise. Serve over brown rice.

To prepare gluten:
Prepare gluten from GLUTEN STEAK recipe using 1/4 recipe only. After boiling gluten, cool and put through meat grinder. Brown in a non-stick fry pan. May sprinkle with a little nutritional yeast flakes.

BLUEBERRY PIE

1 pkg., 20 oz. frozen blueberries or 4 c. fresh
1 c. frozen grape juice concentrate, undiluted
1/4 c. quick cooking tapioca
1 1/2 tsp. coconut flavoring or vanilla
1 1/2 tsp. lemon juice
1/8 tsp. salt
1 baked 9 inch pie crust

Thaw blueberries. Mix grape juice concentrate and tapioca and let stand 5 minutes. Bring to a light boil, stirring often, until tapioca is clear, stir in blueberries and let simmer about 5 minutes. Pour into baked pie crust. Refrigerate until firm. Top with favorite cream topping.

Variation: Use as topping for waffles, crepes or cheesecakes. Use only 2 Tbs. of tapioca.

CORNMEAL BUNS see page 225

VANILLA ICE CREAM see page 271

Nice with Rice

MAIN COURSE
Curry and Vegetables served over
Long Grain Brown Rice

SALAD
"Fresh" Parsley Salad

BREAD
Sprouted Wheat Bread

DESSERT
Deluxe Strawberry Jello
Pear Ice Cream

CURRY

1 large onion, finely chopped
4 cloves garlic, finely chopped
1 1/2 tsp. salt
2 Tbs. CURRY POWDER
1/3 c. tomato paste
3 c. water
Options:
1) tofu
2) GLUTEN STEAK, cubed
3) vegetables: potatoes, carrots, green peas, cauliflower

Saute onions and garlic. Add next four ingredients and lightly boil 5 minutes. Add above options and cook for 20 minutes to 1/2 hour. Serve with cooked brown rice.

CURRY POWDER

1 1/2 Tbs. garlic powder
2 Tbs. turmeric
2 Tbs. coriander, ground
2 Tbs. cumin, ground

Mix together and use as needed.

PARSLEY SALAD

1 1/2 bunches parsley
2 tomatoes, diced
1/2 cucumber, not peeled, chopped
1/2 c. sunflower seeds
1 tsp. salt
2 Tbs. lemon juice
2 Tbs. honey

Chop leaves and ends of parsley and add remaining ingredients. Mix and leave overnight to marinate.

DELUXE STRAWBERRY JELLO

1 c. Emes strawberry flavored gelatin
1 1/2 c. boiling water
3 c. frozen strawberries or any other fruit such as raspberries

Dissolve gelatin into boiling water. Thaw berries, blend and strain to make 2 1/2 c. of juice. May need to add a little water. Add juice to jello. Stir and chill. Save the remaining pulp if you desire.

SPROUTED WHEAT BREAD see page 221

PEAR ICE CREAM see page 272

THIS SPACE FOR YOUR NOTES & RECIPES

_____

_____

_____

_____

_____

_____

_____

_____

_____

_____

_____

_____

_____

_____

_____

_____

_____

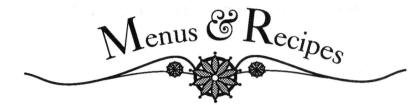

Soup
du Jour

THIS SPACE FOR YOUR NOTES & RECIPES

_____

_____

_____

_____

_____

_____

_____

_____

_____

_____

_____

_____

_____

_____

_____

THIS SPACE FOR YOUR NOTES & RECIPES

_____

_____

_____

_____

_____

_____

_____

_____

_____

_____

_____

_____

_____

_____

_____

_____

SOUPS & SANDWICHES

Spring is a delightful time of the year with the return of the robins, blackbirds and other vacationers. Here and there patches of brown earth melt their way across the gardens and bring into view memories of fresh vegetables. After a winter of root cellar and canning jar meals, something fresh is needed to break the monotony. Even the decorated produce department of the local food chain can't beat something from the garden.

Baby carrots, deep green beet tops, tiny peas, and new potatoes add delicious qualities to homemade soup. You may question the economy of time and money spent on making your own soup, but once you've served a successful bowlful, all the fancy labeling on commercial tins won't entice you for a moment.

During war years, due to the food shortages, many people were forced to grow gardens to augment diminishing food supplies. Those years have been looked upon by medical science historians as productive of good health due to the use of more vegetables and less animal products and refined foods. My grandfather, living in England, loaded his wheel barrow on the weekend, pushed it out of town and grew delicious vegetables for his family on a plot of land procured for that purpose. Perched on the top of the wheel barrow would be one of his children going along to help with weeding and harvesting. What a wonderful education!

Dr. Leo Wattenburg, working at the University of Minnesota School of Medicine, discovered that rats, fed a balanced highly purified diet containing all known vitamins and nutrients, were not able to make certain enzymes in the liver which inactivate cancer-causing chemicals. However when rats were fed a crude diet containing alfalfa they were able to produce the enzymes. Other experiments showed this enzyme increased protection against cancer even when cancer-carrying chemicals were added to their diet. Dr. Wattenburg found that cabbage, brussel sprouts, turnips, broccoli, cauliflower, spinach, dill and celery caused the enzymes to be made but varied in effectiveness according to their freshness and the soil in which they were grown.

In the summer our family favorite is a piping hot bowl of homemade soup and an abundance of fresh vegetables right from the garden. We love to make up sandwiches. Each of us has his own individual preferences. A plate of sliced tomatoes, leaf lettuce, homemade cheese, some homemade mayonnaise, onions, etc. is all it takes to bring enough creativity to satisfy everyone's appetite. Here are menus for you to enjoy your vegetables fresh from the garden or store.

Hints for Soup

1. Always have water boiling before adding vegetables.

2. Put seasoning in while water is boiling.

3. Put all raw vegetables in at the same time.

4. Use parsley as a basic ingredient.
5. Use garlic as a basic ingredient.

6. Shredded carrots are nice.

7. Use 2 T. olive oil for a large pot of soup.

8. Make a cream sauce to add when the soup has finished cooking by blending smooth: 1 c. of cashews to 2 c. water. Then add this to the soup.

9. Use herbs such as bay leaves, thyme, sweet basil for "dry bean" soups.

Soup du Jour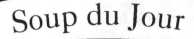

SOUP OF THE DAY
Tomato Vegetable Soup

BREAD & SPREAD
**June's Heritage Spread or
Aunt Tilly's Pickle Sandwiches**

SALAD PLATE
Tray of Lettuce, Tomatoes, Cucumbers

DESSERT
Popcorn, Peanuts & Raisins

TOMATO VEGETABLE SOUP

8 c. water
1 bay leaf
2 Tbs. CHICKEN STYLE SEASONING
1 Tbs. dried parsley flakes
1 tsp. summer savory
1 tsp. garlic salt
1 tsp. salt
1/4 c. pearled barley
1 chopped onion
2 med. potatoes, chopped fine
2 grated carrots
2 stalks celery, chopped fine
2 c. TOMATO SOUP or tomato juice thickened with 2 Tbs. flour

Bring water to a boil in a covered saucepan. Add next seven ingredients. Lightly boil 20 minutes. Add vegetables and simmer until tender. Add tomato soup. Simmer and serve.

Variation: May add shredded cabbage, green beans, zucchini, beet or spinach greens.

JUNE'S HERITAGE SANDWICH SPREAD

1 lg. onion
1 clove garlic
1/2 c. raw, soaked garbanzo beans
2/3 c. walnuts
1 c. water
2 c. gluten flour
2 1/2 tsp. salt
1/4 tsp. sage

Broth:
2 1/2 c. boiling water
1 1/2 Tbs. Marmite or 2 Tbs. soy sauce

Blend first five ingredients. Mix gluten flour, salt and sage. Combine with first set of ingredients. Put in greased casserole. Set in pan of hot water. Pour broth mixture over. Cover and bake at 350° for 2 hours. Uncover for last 30 minutes.

AUNT TILLY'S PICKLE SANDWICH

1 qt. dill pickles
Mayonnaise

Thoroughly drain pickles overnight. Shred and mix with mayonnaise. Spread on bread.

Soup du Jour

SOUP OF THE DAY
Frenchies Tomato Soup with Rice

BREAD & SPREAD
**Chicken Style Lunch Meat Loaf on Rye Bread
Lo Cal Mustard**

SALAD PLATE
**Marinated Onions
Beef Steak Tomato Slices**

DESSERT
Carob Chip Cookies #1 or #2

FRENCHIES TOMATO SOUP

8 c. V-8 juice or seasoned tomato juice
2 Tbs. olive oil
1/3 c. + 1 Tbs. flour
1 tsp. salt
2 Tbs. honey

Mix flour with 1 c. of juice. Bring to boil remaining ingredients. Add juice with flour, stirring until thickened. Put in 2 c. cooked rice for tomato rice soup.

CHICKEN STYLE LUNCHEON MEAT

1/2 c. soy flour
1/2 c. cornmeal
1/2 c. cashews
1 1/2 c. water
1 Tbs. CHICKEN STYLE SEASONING
1/4 c. yeast flakes
3/4 c. gluten flour
1 tsp. salt
1/2 c. onions, chopped, optional
1/2 c. green pepper, chopped, optional

Whiz the first four ingredients in blender until smooth and creamy. Now mix all ingredients together in a bowl. Put in a greased, 20 oz. can and cover with foil. Next steam in a steamer with water half way up the side of the can for 1 1/2 hour. Watch periodically to see that water does not boil away. Add water as needed.

Another way to cook is to put a jar lid, at least 1/4 inch thick, in saucepan. Place can with recipe in it on top of the lid. Add water in pan half way up the side of the can and lightly boil 1 1/2 hours.

LO-CAL MUSTARD

1 clove garlic
1/3 c. lemon juice
1/2 c. water
1-2 Tbs. oil
1 tsp. turmeric
1/2 tsp. salt
1/4 c. flour

Put last five ingredients in blender to mix. Put in saucepan and cook until thickened. Return to blender and add garlic and while whizzing, slowly add the lemon juice. Refrigerate to chill and thicken.

RYE BREAD see page 222

MARINATED ONIONS see page 237

CAROB CHIP COOKIES see page 247

Soup du Jour

SOUP OF THE DAY
Borscht #1 or #2

BREAD & SPREAD
Crackers & Jack Cheese
or Bonanza Bean Dip

SALAD PLATE
Carrot Sticks
Olives

DESSERT
Carob Fudge

BEET SOUP, BORSCHT # 1

2 onions or leeks, chopped
2 Tbs. olive oil
6 c. water
1 c. dried navy beans
4 med. beets
1/4 head cabbage, shredded
6 carrots, finely chopped
2 Tbs. CHICKEN STYLE SEASONING
2 Tbs. fresh chopped dill
1 tsp. salt
1 tsp. garlic salt
5 c. tomato juice
1 c. nuts, blanched almonds or cashews
1 Tbs. flour

Soak beans at least 6 hours in 3 c. water. Drain. Saute onions in olive oil in large saucepan. When onions are tender, add 6 c. water and beans to pan. Cover. Lightly boil 1 hour. Chop three beets and add to soup. Continue to cook 15 minutes. Shred other beet and set aside. Put cabbage into a bowl. Pour some boiling water over it and let stand. Add carrots to soup. Continue to cook 15 minutes. Drain cabbage. Add cabbage, shredded beet and seasonings to soup. Blend smooth 1 c. tomato juice with nuts and flour. Stir into soup with remaining juice. While stirring return to a light boil and continue to simmer about 10 minutes or until vegetables and beans are tender. Serve.

RUSSIAN BORSCHT # 2

10 c. boiling water
1/2 c. canned tomatoes
5-6 peeled potatoes, cubed
1 lg. carrot, chopped
2 sm. peeled beets, cubed
1 onion, chopped
1-2 Tbs. salt
3/4 c. onion, chopped
3 c. canned tomatoes, chopped
3 c. cabbage, chopped
1/2 c. corn, optional
1 1/2 c. diced raw potatoes
1/2 c. tomato sauce
2 Tbs. olive oil
2 c. shredded cooked cabbage
1/2 tsp. dill seed
1 tsp. garlic salt
1/2 c. chopped green pepper

Combine and cook until tender first seven ingredients. Mash. Saute onion and 3 c. tomatoes. Saute cabbage in small amount of water and cook until tender. Combine all ingredients. Bring to a boil. Reduce heat. Add remaining ingredients. Simmer until vegetables are done. Serve.

CAROB FUDGE see page 252 and 253

Soup du Jour

SOUP OF THE DAY
Corn Chowder

BREAD & SPREAD
Chicken Salad Sandwiches

SALAD PLATE
Fresh Ice-Berg Lettuce
Radishes, Cucumbers, Black Olives,
Bread & Butter Pickles

DESSERT
Pear Tapioca
Trail Mix (Carob Chips/Peanuts/Raisins)

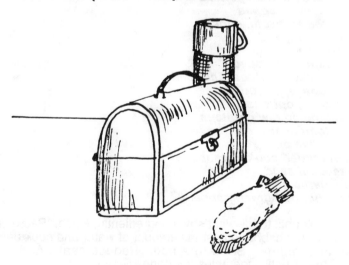

CORN CHOWDER

Kettle: 1/3 to 1/2 full of boiling water
sauteed onions
CHICKEN STYLE SEASONING, optional
salt
parsley
potatoes, chopped
carrots, grated
celery, chopped
1 Tbs. oil, optional
corn

Cook vegetables in boiling water until tender. Add corn. Make a cream sauce by blending smooth equal portions of cashews and water. For 4 c. of soup add 1 c. of cream sauce. Heat and serve. Try using equal proportions of potatoes and corn.

CHICKEN SALAD SANDWICHES

1 recipe CHICKEN LOAF
DILL PICKLES
celery
onions
olives
TOFU MAYONNAISE

Grind chilled Chicken Loaf through meat grinder or mash with fork. Chop remaining ingredients and mix in with mayonnaise to desired consistency. Spread on favorite bread. Try bagels, or pocket bread. Serve with favorite lettuce.

PEAR TAPIOCA

1/3 c. quick cooking tapioca
1/4 c. lemon juice
1 c. pear juice from canned pears
2 c. pineapple juice
5 pear halves, drained

Cook the tapioca with the juices until clear. Let cool 5 minutes. Pour mixture into individual bowls. Chill. Place a pear half on top of each bowl of pudding.

Soup du Jour

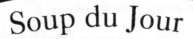

SOUP OF THE DAY
Cauliflower Soup

BREAD & SPREAD
Sesame Seed Buns
Nuteena or Hommus Tahini

SALAD PLATE
Romaine Lettuce
Baby Dills
Tomatoes
Relish
Lo Cal Mustard

DESSERT
Hay Stack Cookies

CAULIFLOWER SOUP

2 c. cauliflower, chopped
1 c. peas
2/3 c. blanched almonds or cashews
1 Tbs. CHICKEN STYLE SEASONING

Follow the recipe and ingredients for TOMATO VEGETABLE SOUP but omit the tomato soup and summer savory. After soup has simmered and is tender add cauliflower. Bring to boil and simmer 10 minutes. Add peas. Blend almonds or cashews and chicken style seasoning with 1 c. water to make a smooth sauce. Pour into soup. Heat and serve.

NUTEENA-LIKE SPREAD

1-15 oz. size can garbanzo beans, drained, save juice
2/3 c. chopped olives
1/3 c. garbanzo juice
1/3 c. peanut butter
1 1/2 Tbs. tomato paste
1/4 tsp. onion powder
1 tsp. lemon juice

Mash garbanzos thoroughly in bowl or blend lightly. Add remaining ingredients and mix well. Delicious topped with onions and sprouts served on crackers.

HOMMUS TAHINI

15 oz. can garbanzo beans, drained
1/2 c. sesame seeds, lightly toasted and blended dry
1 clove garlic, optional
1/2 tsp. salt
1 Tbs. parsley, optional
3 Tbs. lemon juice

Blend all but parsley with just enough bean broth or water to blend smooth, about 1/2 c. Stir in chopped parsley. Serve as a spread.

LO-CAL MUSTARD see page 211

HAYSTACK COOKIES see page 249

Soup du Jour

SOUP OF THE DAY
**Split Pea Chowder
or Split Pea Soup**

BREAD & SPREAD
**Sprouted Wheat Bread
Avocado
Popcorn**

SALAD PLATE
**Carrot Sticks
Pickles
Celery Sticks
Green Olives**

DESSERT
Polynesian Bars

SPLIT PEA CHOWDER

6 c. water
1/2 c. brown rice
2 c. split peas
2 tsp. salt
1 c. sauteed onions
1/2 c. finely diced carrots
1/2 c. finely diced celery or minced celery tops
1 tsp. sweet basil
chopped potatoes, optional

Add rice and peas to rapidly boiling water in large kettle. Cover. Bring to full boil and let cook 1 1/2 hours. Add remaining ingredients. Cook 15-20 minutes. Vegetables should be crisp yet tender.

SPLIT PEA SOUP

4 c. water
2 c. split peas
1 sliced onion
1/4 c. chopped fresh parsley, optional
1/4 tsp. thyme
1/4 tsp. rosemary
1 bay leaf
1 Tbs. CHICKEN STYLE SEASONING or 1 tsp. salt and 1/2 tsp.
*   basil*
salt to taste

Simmer peas and water until soft, 45 minutes in covered saucepan. Add other ingredients and boil gently for 10 minutes. Blend soup in blender. Dilute to desired consistency with water.

SPROUTED WHEAT BREAD see page 221

PICKLES see page 210

POLYNESIAN BARS see page 251

Soup du Jour

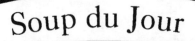

SOUP OF THE DAY
Lentil Soup

BREAD & SPREAD
Pizza Pockets

SALAD PLATE
Cabbage Salad

DESSERT
Granola Bars

LENTIL SOUP

2 c. lentils, uncooked
onions
potatoes
tomatoes
grated carrots
bay leaves
thyme
sweet basil
oil
1 1/2-2 tsp. salt
1 qt. canned tomatoes

Add onions and lentils to 6 1/2 c. water and boil for 45 minutes in covered saucepan. Add remaining ingredients except tomatoes. When it returns to a boil, add tomatoes, then simmer until done, about 20-30 minutes.

PIZZA POCKETS

1 recipe TOMATO SAUCE from page 93
Add any of your favorites such as pineapple, tofu and
   PIMENTO CHEESE to the sauce

Dough:
1 tsp. salt
5 c. whole wheat and white flour combined or all whole wheat
2 c. warm water
1 Tbs. sugar or honey
1 Tbs. yeast

Dissolve yeast in water and honey. Put dry ingredients in a bowl and make a well. Put dissolved yeast into center and mix and knead. Roll out dough 1/4 in. thick. Cut into squares 3x3. Put some sauce in middle and then bring up 4 corners and pinch each seam. Let rise a few minutes and bake 30 minutes at 350°. Can reheat or eat cold. Great for lunches and traveling.

CABBAGE SALAD

chopped cabbage
1 c. shredded carrot
1 c. unsweetened crushed pineapple
1/2 c. nuts
salt to taste
MAYONNAISE

Toss together well.

GRANOLA BARS see page 251

Soup du Jour

SOUP OF THE DAY
Vegetable Lima Bean Soup

BREAD & SPREAD
Grilled Cheese Sandwiches #1, #2

SALAD PLATE
Bread & Butter Pickles
Buttercrunch Lettuce
Baby Green Onions

DESSERT
Sesame Fingers

VEGETABLE LIMA BEAN SOUP

2 c. lima beans, dried
8 c. water
1 Tbs. CHICKEN STYLE SEASONING
1 c. frozen peas
1/2 c. soy alphabet noodles, optional

Bring water and beans to a light boil in a covered saucepan. Cook until soft, about 2 1/2-3 hours. (Or, may soak beans in 6 c. of water over night, drain; then lightly boil until soft with 5 1/2 c.-about 2 1/2 hours.) Using a separate saucepan, follow the list of ingredients and directions for TOMATO VEGETABLE SOUP, omitting ingredients 3-7. When beans are done, blend them with chicken seasoning and as little water as possible to make a cream, add to soup. May leave some beans whole to add to soup. Add peas and noodles. Simmer and serve.

GRILLED CHEESE SANDWICHES # 1

1 c. water
3/4 c. cashews
1 Tbs. sesame seeds
1 1/4 tsp. salt
1/4 tsp. ground dill seed
1/8 tsp. garlic powder
3 Tbs. yeast flakes
1/2 c. pimento, 4 oz. jar
1 Tbs. arrowroot powder or cornstarch
1/3 c. lemon juice

Blend all ingredients until smooth. Cook, stirring constantly, until thick. Spread whole wheat bread with cheese filling and a slice of tomato if desired. Spread CORN BUTTER on outside of bread and toast in skillet on both sides, or in a small bowl mix 2 Tbs. cornstarch, 1 c. water, 1/4 tsp. salt. Dip the outsides of the sandwiches in this mixture and place on greased cookie sheet. Bake in oven at 350° about 10-15 minutes on each side. Delicious!

GRILLED CHEESE SANDWICHES # 2
JACK CHEESE recipe on page 205
Slice cheese on bread and grill in oven.

Soup du Jour

SOUP OF THE DAY
Eileen's Favorite Cucumber Soup

BREAD & SPREAD
Super Sandwich Soymeat Slices
Whole Wheat Toast
Lo-Cal Mustard
Ketchup

SALAD PLATE
Carrot Sticks
Dill Pickles
Great Northern Tomatoes/Long English Cucumbers

DESSERT
Fruity Chews
Apricot Yummies

EILEEN'S FAVORITE CUCUMBER SOUP

1 med. onion
1 1/2 tsp. olive oil
1/4 c. flour
1/2 tsp. salt, or to taste
4 c. water
2 Tbs. CHICKEN STYLE SEASONING or 1 1/2 tsp. salt and 1 1/2
*   tsp. basil*
1 stalk celery, chopped fine
2 med. carrots, chopped fine
2 med. potatoes, chopped fine
5 med. cucumbers, peeled, cored, diced
1 c. cooked rice
2 Tbs. lemon juice
2 bay leaves
1/2 c. almonds or cashews
2/3 c. water
1/4 c. fresh parsley

Saute onion in olive oil. Add flour and salt. Stir in water and chicken seasoning. When boiling add next three vegetables. Simmer for 10 minutes. Add cucumbers and simmer 10 minutes. Pour half of mixture in blender and whiz until smooth. Pour back into soup and add rice, lemon juice and bay leaves. Simmer another 20 minutes. Blend nuts and water until smooth. Add to soup and stir in parsley. Simmer and serve.

SUPER SANDWICH SOYMEAT SLICES

1 c. dry soybeans
2 c. water
1 c. tomato juice
1/2 c. peanut butter
1/2 med. onion
1 stalk celery
1/4 c. yeast flakes
1/4 c. soy sauce
garlic salt to taste
1 c. cornmeal
2 tsp. salt

Soak beans overnight in 4 c. water. Drain. Blend smooth soaked soybeans and 2 c. water. Add remaining ingredients except the cornmeal and blend until smooth. Remove from blender, add cornmeal. Pour into oiled 16-20 oz. cans, filling 2/3 full, and steam for 2 hours or longer. Steam in large kettle about 1/3 full of water when cans are set in it. Keep water simmering with lid on. When done, let cool in can. Remove. Chill then slice.

LO-CAL MUSTARD see page 211
KETCHUP see page 212
FRUITY CHEWS see page 269
APRICOT YUMMIES see page 269

Soup du Jour

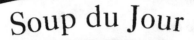

SOUP OF THE DAY
Cream of Potato Soup

BREAD & SPREAD
Pocket Bread
Eggless Salad Sandwiches

SALAD PLATE
Fried Tomatoes
Fried Lettuce
Mayonnaise
Baco Bits

DESSERT
Carob Chips or
Peanut Butter Cookies

CREAM OF POTATO SOUP

1 c. diced potatoes
1/2 c. chopped onion
1/2 tsp. salt or to taste
1 c. chopped celery
1 c. water
2 c. CASHEW OR ALMOND MILK
1 Tbs. flour
1 Tbs. olive oil
chopped, fresh parsley

Cook potatoes, onion and celery in salted water until tender. Do not drain, mash. Combine and blend milk, flour and 1 Tbs. olive oil and stir into hot liquid; simmer together 5 minutes stirring constantly. Top each serving with chopped parsley.

POCKET BREAD

Using favorite bread dough recipe mix and knead the dough. Divide into balls the size of walnuts and roll into a 1/8 in. circle. Place on clean cloth and let rise 1/2 hour. Preheat oven to 400°. Put a few pocket breads on a cooling rack at a time and put in oven. Now watch through the glass as it rises. Bake just a few minutes until just begins to turn golden. Not crispy hard. Take out and put in a basket lined with clean towel. Cover until ready to serve. Kids love to help make these!

EGGLESS SALAD SANDWICHES

1 lb. tofu, rinsed and mashed
2-3 Tbs. CHICKEN STYLE SEASONING
1 sm. minced onion
1 stalk celery, chopped fine
2 Tbs. chopped BREAD AND BUTTER PICKLES, optional
salt to taste

Mix in enough TOFU MAYONNAISE to get desired consistency.

MAYONNAISE see page 202 or 203

PEANUT BUTTER CAROB CHIP COOKIES see page 248

CAROB CHIP COOKIES see page 247

THIS SPACE FOR YOUR NOTES & RECIPES

_____

_____

_____

_____

_____

_____

_____

_____

_____

_____

_____

_____

_____

_____

_____

_____

Menus & Recipes

Family
Fun

THIS SPACE FOR YOUR NOTES & RECIPES

_____

_____

_____

_____

_____

_____

_____

_____

_____

_____

_____

_____

_____

_____

_____

HOLIDAY SPECIALS

In the Scriptures there are numerous references to the evils of over indulgence and the importance of maintaining a clear mind capable of appreciating personal responsibility and opportunity. Along with these warnings are obvious accounts of genuine happiness and enjoyment of different scenes and celebration. The marriage feast, the feast of tabernacles and other like gatherings brought friends and families together for innocent social communion. Today in this world caught up with pleasure seeking, dissipation and merriment, there is still a place for the family celebration and social enjoyment to be shared at festive occasions.

"Let several families living in a city or village unite and leave the occupations which have taxed them physically and mentally and make an excursion into the country, to the side of a fine lake or to a nice grove, where the scenery of nature is beautiful. They should provide themselves with plain hygienic food, the very best fruits and grains, and spread their table under the shade of some tree or under the canopy of heaven. The ride, the exercise and the scenery will quicken the appetite and they can enjoy a repast which kings might envy." Counsel on Diet & Foods page 87.

"Those who understand the laws of health and who are governed by principle, will shun the extremes, both of indulgence and restriction. Their diet is chosen not for the mere gratification of appetite, but for the upbuilding of the body. They seek to preserve every power in the best condition for highest service to God and man. The appetite is under the control of reason and conscience and they are rewarded with health of body and mind. While they do not urge their views offensively upon others, their example is a testimony in favor of right principle. These persons have a wide influence for good."

"There is real common sense in dietetic reform. The subject should be studied broadly and deeply, and no one should criticize others because their practice is not in all things in harmony with his own." Ministry of Healing page 319.

In our society stress is constantly wearing away our nervous energy and eroding our digestive ability. News casts laden with the fights and follies of our fellow men season our daily communications and there needs to be a place and time where these annoyances are laid aside, where the prayer of faith and thanksgiving is heard, and courage, hope and trust flavor the conversations. The holiday celebration is an excellent time to practice an event that grows into a daily routine.

Family Fun

NOTHING BEATS A PIZZA PARTY
Crusty Pizza Crust with Tomato Sauce
Crumbled Tofu
Melty or Jack Cheese
Add your favorite toppings:
Olives
Pineapple
Mushrooms
Baco Bits
Onion Rings
Green Pepper
Tomato Slices

SERVED WITH:
Gisele's Greek Salad
Dill Pickles, Olives

DESSERT
Brad's Frozen Delight
Dried Fruit Ball Arrangement

PIZZA DOUGH

5 c. flour, white and whole wheat
1 tsp. salt
2 1/2 c. warm water
1 Tbs. sugar
1 Tbs. yeast

Mix flour and salt together. Dissolve sugar and yeast in warm water. Make a well in flour and pour yeast mixture into flour. Mix and knead. Roll out onto cookie sheets, makes 2 cookie sheets. Spread tomato sauce on pizza, see spaghetti sauce below. Crumble tofu and pour on MELTY CHEESE or JACK CHEESE. Then put on favorite toppings and bake at 350° for 35-40 minutes.

SPAGHETTI TOMATO SAUCE, revised for use on pizza

28 oz. tomatoes, canned or 3 1/2 c. fresh, peeled
6 oz. tomato paste
2 Tbs. sweetening, optional
1 tsp. basil
1 tsp. salt
1 tsp. paprika
1 bay leaf
1/2 tsp. cumin, optional
1/4 tsp. dry minced garlic or 1 tsp. fresh

Simmer over low-med. heat until flavors are blended and sauce is thick. Remove bay leaf. Tomato sauce is always better the next day. Flavors blend better.

JACK CHEESE

1/2 c. water
1/4 c. Emes unflavored gelatin
3/4 c. boiling water
1 c. cashews, raw
1/4 c. nutritional yeast flakes
1 1/2 tsp. salt
1 tsp. onion powder
1/4 tsp. garlic powder
1/4 c. lemon juice
2 Tbs. finely grated carrot or red pepper to color

Soak gelatin in the 1/2 c. water in blender, while assembling remaining ingredients. Pour boiling water over soaked gelatin and whiz briefly to dissolve. Cool slightly. Add cashews and liquefy thoroughly. Add remaining ingredients. Liquefy until mixture is creamy. Pour into container, cool slightly. Cover and refrigerate overnight before using. Slice and serve.

MELTY CHEESE see page 206
GISELE'S GREEK SALAD see page 239
PICKLES see page 210, 211
BRAD'S FROZEN DELIGHT see page 272
DRIED FRUIT BALL see page 270
FRUIT CANDY see page 270

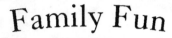

Family Fun

CHEF'S CHOICES
According to Age & Taste
Waffles & Favorite Sauces
Hamburgers & French Fries
Haystacks
Stroganoff
Spaghetti
Pizza
Older Generation - "Favorite Meat & Potato Meal"

DESSERT
5 Minute Orange Cake or
Boiled Raisin Cake with added fruit or
Waffle Cake

BOILED RAISIN CAKE

2 c. raisins
3 c. water
1/2 c. warm water
1 Tbs. honey
2 Tbs. active dry yeast
1 3/4 c. raisin water
2/3 c. raw sugar or 1/2 c. honey
1 Tbs. vanilla
1 Tbs. grated ORANGE RIND
1 c. walnuts
1 tsp. salt
1/2 c. whole wheat pastry flour
1 c. additional flour, whole wheat or unbleached white
1 1/2 c. unbleached white flour
soaked raisins
1 c. chopped walnuts
anise or coriander, optional

Boil raisins and water together for 5 minutes. Drain off water and save to replace some of the water in recipe. Dissolve yeast and honey in warm water. Blend smooth next 7 ingredients in blender. Add to yeast mixture stirring as little as possible. Fold in additional flour and let rise 15-20 minutes, not more. Then fold in remaining flour. Add remaining ingredients. Prepare cake pan by cutting waxed paper to fit, and grease paper or oil and flour cake pan. Fill pan 1/2 full. Let rise in pan 10 minutes, not more. Bake at 350° for 35-40 minutes.

VARIATIONS:
#1 - BANANA NUT CAKE

Replace raisins with 2 c. mashed banana. Leave out 3 c. water. Use 1 3/4 c. plain water in blended ingredients. If icing desired, try roasting 2/3 c. nuts, almonds or cashews, and making a thick nut butter. Add some melted honey and vanilla and perhaps orange flavoring or rind. Drizzle over cake before serving.

#2 - Put different dried fruit, in batter as well as the raisins, such as dried papaya, and dried pineapple. Ice with melted carob chips.

5 MINUTE ORANGE CAKE see page 256

WAFFLE CAKE see page 258

Family Fun

MAIN COURSE IDEAS
Gluten Steaks or Gluten Pinwheels
Cranberry Sauce

POTATO IDEAS
Scalloped Potatoes or Rice Potatoes

VEGETABLES
Baked Squash or Corn on the Cob & Broccoli Spears

SALAD
**Tossed Green Salad or Bok Choy Salad
with Broccoli Stems, unpeeled**

DESSERT
**Hot Blachinda's or
Pumpkin Pie
Pear Vanilla Ice Cream**

GLUTEN PINWHEELS

1 recipe pie crust dough
hot mashed potatoes
GLUTEN STEAKS, ground

Make pie crust and roll in rectangle shape. Spread with hot mashed potatoes. Then spread seasoned gluten burger. Roll up as a jelly roll and cut 1 1/2 in. thick. Place on greased cookie sheets. Bake at 350° until crust is brown, about 30 minutes. Serve with gravy.

CRANBERRY SAUCE

1 package cranberries
1 large apple
1/2 orange, including peeling
1/2-1/3 c. honey

If possible freeze cranberries first. Blend a few at a time in blender, so they don't mush. Grate apple. Blend orange including peel or just use orange juice. If you do not have a blender, chop like you would parsley. Add melted honey.

PUMPKIN PIE

1/2 c. honey
1/4 c. flour
2 c. cooked pumpkin or squash
1/2 tsp. salt
1/2 tsp. vanilla
1 1/2 c. nut milk
1/2 tsp. anise

Blend thoroughly and pour into unbaked pie shell. Bake 450° for 10 minutes and then 325° for 30-40 minutes.

BLACHINDA see page 260

VANILLA ICE CREAM see page 271

Family Fun

MAIN COURSE IDEAS
**Chicken Loaf or Cashew Loaf,
Manicotti or Bread Dressing**

POTATO IDEAS
**Tilly's Potatoes/Mary's Brown Gravy
Oven Potato Surprise/Onion Gravy
Stuffed Baked Potato/Soy Cream Cheese**

VEGETABLES
**Brussels Sprouts with Melty Cheese or Jack Cheese
Creamed Corn, Pineapple Yams**

SALAD
**Broccoli Cauliflower Salad/Vegetable Jelly Salad
Salad & Pickle Plates/Cranberry Sauce**

DESSERT
**Plum Pudding
Pear Cream, Ice Cream or Hot Lemon Sauce
Cookie Plate of Christmas Candy Cake & Carob Kisses**

CHICKEN LOAF

4 c. ground soy chicken
1 tsp. CHICKEN STYLE SEASONING, optional
1 c. bread crumbs
1 c. rich soy milk or nut cream
1 med. onion
1 c. celery
1 tsp. sage

Saute last 3 ingredients. Mix altogether and bake in an oiled loaf pan at 350° for 1 hour or until firm and brown.

Note: The Soy Chicken is a frozen, commercially prepared meat substitute that can be purchased in healthfood stores.

SPECIAL CHRISTMAS CANDY CAKE

1 1/2 c. brown sugar or honey
3 c. sifted white flour
1 tsp. salt
2 c. FLAX SEED JELL
1 Tbs. vanilla
2 tsp. almond flavoring
3 c. or 1 lb. currants
4 c. or 1 lb. soft chopped dates
3 1/2 c. or 1 lb. cherries
3 c. or 1 lb. raisins
3 c. or 1 lb. dried pineapple
3 c. or 1 lb. walnuts or almonds
3 c. or 1 lb. dried papaya

Mix first 6 ingredients to make batter. Work in remaining ingredients gently with your hands. Heap into four 7 inch loaf pans prepared as follows: Cut grocery bags to fit pans and grease well. Bake at 300° for 1 hour, covered lightly with aluminum foil and then 10-20 minutes uncovered. Remove from oven. Peel off liner as soon as cool enough to handle. Let cool. Wrap in wax paper, then aluminum foil and refrigerate. Keeps all year!
Note: For the cherries, drizzle some honey on frozen or canned cherries and slow cook for several hours until cooked down but not hard and dry. Or bake in the oven in a glass dish at 250°. You may also use dried cherries. If you don't have dried pineapple, you can use canned pineapple chunks, but they should be cooked in oven the same as cherries.

Variation: May vary dried fruit according to preference and availability.

FLAX SEED JEL

2 c. water
6 Tbs. flax seed

Boil for 5 minutes. Strain and let cool in refrigerator overnight.
Note: 1/4 c. flax seed jell can be used in place of one egg in some baked goods.

Family Fun

AT THE FIRE PIT
Tofu Wieners & Hot Dog Buns
Roasted Corn & Potato & Onion Wedges
Gluten Jerky
Dough on Stick

GARNISHES
Relish, Chopped Onions
Ketchup, Jack Cheese & Mustard

DESSERT
Carob Clusters & Orange Juice

ROASTED CORN, POTATOES

Prepare Potatoes:
Scrub potatoes. Cut wedges in potatoes and put slices of onion in them. Wrap with foil.
Prepare corn:
Soak corn in salted water for 1 hour in husks. Build fire. Develop bed of coals. Scrape away coals into a pile. Place corn in husk and wrapped potatoes on hot ground. Cover with ashes. Check after 30 minutes. If not done, keep checking every 5 minutes until done.

DOUGH ON STICK

whole wheat flour
unbleached white flour
cornmeal
salt

Prepare at home equal portions of whole wheat, unbleached flour and corn meal. Add a little salt.
Campout:
Find in forest big sticks about an inch and a half in diameter and then fine skinny sticks, the kind you would use for marshmallows. Put desired amount of flour mixture in bowl. Add enough water to make a dough the consistency of soft bread dough. Take a portion and pat into a thin pancake and stretch it around the big stick, on the top too. Cook in fire until forms a golden brown crust. Don't burn. Pull gently off stick. Now take the smaller stick and poke it through the middle of dough, holding vertically to the fire so the inside will finish baking. Then stuff it with your favorite filler such as peanut butter, jam or honey, beans or tofu wiener. Such fun!

GLUTEN JERKY

Make gluten mix. Use GLUTEN STEAKS recipe, page 67.
Cut gluten into thin strips. Drop into boiling broth. Cook slowly until juice is almost completely evaporated. Add 1-3 Tbs. liquid smoke, depending on personal preference. Stir well, simmer 5 minutes and let cool. Lay strips on cookie sheet. Bake at 250-300° until dried to preferred consistency. Turn often, takes about 5-6 hours to get dry.

CAROB CLUSTERS see page 253

Family Fun

THERMOS OR COOLER
Favorite Soup in Thermos/Crackers on the side
Left over Stroganoff & Rice
heated to stuff in Pocket Bread
Potato Salad
Cereal in Thermos

SANDWICH
Any of the Sandwich Fillings in book such as:
Tofu Egg Salad Sandwich
Super Sandwich Soyameat
Pizza Pockets etc.
Cheese, Pickle, Tomato or Onion Sandwich
Tofu Bologna, Peanut Butter & Jam

SALAD
Any Fruit in Season
Celery & Carrot Sticks/Watermelon

DESSERT
Carob Rice Cakes/Trail Mix/Popcorn
Fruit Leather/Cookies or Squares

CEREAL THERMOS METHOD

1 c. cereal to 3 c. water and 1/2 tsp. salt

In the evening pour boiling water into thermos bottle to heat the lining. Pour water out. Add grains, salt and boiling water. Screw lid on tightly and lay on side. Cereal will be ready to eat following morning.

POCKET BREAD

Using favorite bread dough recipe mix and knead the dough. Divide into balls the size of walnuts and roll into a 1/8 inch thick circle. Place on clean cloth and let rise 1/2 hour. Preheat oven to 400°. Put a few pocket breads on a cooling rack at a time and put in oven. Now watch through the glass as it rises. Bake just a few minutes until just begins to turn golden. Not crispy hard. Take out and put in a basket lined with clean towel. Cover until ready to serve. Kids love to help make these!

PIZZA POCKETS

1 recipe TOMATO SAUCE from page 93 or 173
Add any of your favorites such as pineapple, tofu and
*   PIMENTO CHEESE to the sauce*

Dough:
1 tsp. salt
5 c. whole wheat and white flour combined or all whole wheat
2 c. warm water
1 Tbs. sugar or honey
1 Tbs. yeast

Dissolve yeast in water and honey. Put dry ingredients in a bowl and make a well. Put dissolved yeast into center and mix and knead. Roll out dough 1/4 in. thick. Cut into squares 3x3. Put some sauce in middle and then bring up 4 corners and pinch each seam. Let rise a few minutes and bake 30 minutes at 350°. Can reheat or eat cold. Great for lunches and traveling.

CAROB RICE CAKES

Rice Cakes
Carob Chips

Place rice cakes on cookie sheet. Place small handful of carob chips in center. Put in 300° oven, watch carefully and as soon as carob chips are soft, spread with knife and serve. So fast and yummy. Best when cool.

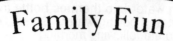

Family Fun

TEA FOR TWO & ETC.
Slushies
Pop
Swamp Water
Hot Peppermint Apple Tea
Tomato V5 Juice
Blending Fun

SLUSHIES

1/2 c. water
1 1/2 tsp. honey or to taste
2 Tbs. frozen fruit juice concentrate or 1 c. whole frozen fruit
    or about 1 tsp. of extract such as root beer-vary to taste
2-3 c. finely chopped ice

Blend all ingredients except ice. Slowly add ice blending well. Pour into glasses and serve immediately.

POP

Simply mix favorite fruit juices and natural mineral water. Try your hand at creating an original.

SWAMP WATER

8 c. orange juice
1-2 tsp. root beer extract
1/4 tsp. lemon juice
3 c. mineral water

Mix together. Chill.

HOT PEPPERMINT APPLE TEA

4 c. peppermint tea
4 c. apple juice
2 Tbs. lemon juice

Heat and serve.

TOMATO V5 JUICE

2 gal. chopped fresh tomatoes
1/2 head of celery
1 green pepper
1-2 chopped onions
2-3 cloves garlic
parsley
Salt, optional

Bring all ingredients to boil in covered sauce pan and simmer until tomatoes are cooked. Take out big pieces of vegetables. Run through press or juicer. Can as usual.

BLENDING:

O.J.-P.J. FREEZE

1/2 c. orange juice
1/4 c. pineapple juice
5 ice cubes
1/8 tsp. coconut extract

Blend and serve.

PINA COLADA

1 c. pineapple juice
5 ice cubes
1/8 tsp. coconut extract

Blend and serve.

STRAWBERRY FROTHIE

1 c. pineapple juice
1 c. frozen strawberries
5 ice cubes
1/4 tsp. vanilla
1-2 Tbs. soy milk, powder, optional

Blend and serve.

GRAPE PIZZANGY

1 c. grape juice
2 tsp. lime juice
5 ice cubes
2 tsp. lemon juice

Blend and serve.

THIS SPACE FOR YOUR NOTES & RECIPES

_____

_____

_____

_____

_____

_____

_____

_____

_____

_____

_____

_____

_____

_____

_____

Family Fun

LITTLE THINGS THAT COUNT
Fruit Leather
Stuffed Dates
Butterfly Sandwiches
Bagels
Gopher Pockets
Carob Rice Cakes
Christmas Nuts & Bolts
Trail Mix
Frozen Grapes

FRUIT LEATHER

Any fresh fruit or combination of fruit may be used. Blend fruit smooth. Place wax paper or plastic wrap onto drying screen. Tape edges down. Pour fruit on to covered trays. Place in dehydrator. When almost dry, remove paper by turning the fruit over on the screen and continue drying. Children love it like candy. I often add applesauce to give it creamy texture. Raspberries are pretty seedy by themselves. Some honey may need to be added.

STUFFED DATES

Toasted almonds
Walnuts
Peanut butter

Stuff dates with one of the suggestions. This is a delicious quick dessert.

BUTTERFLY SANDWICHES

Place a pickle body between sandwich wings. Add carrot curls for antennae.

GOPHER POCKETS

Do your little gophers have a sweet tooth? Fill their pockets! Spread a thin layer of peanut butter and honey inside a pita bread pocket. Add a few chopped dates or figs. Fill it up with sliced bananas. "Go-pher" it!

CAROB RICE CAKES

Rice Cakes
Carob Chips

Place rice cakes on cookie sheet. Place small handful of carob chips in center. Put in 300° oven, watch carefully and as soon as carob chips are soft, spread with knife and serve. So fast and yummy. Best when cool.

CHRISTMAS NUTS & BOLTS

1 lb. of mixed nuts
1 box shreddies or wheat chex
1 box cheerios
2 boxes rice chex
1 box corn bran
2 bags pretzels
1/2 c. olive oil
2 tsp. seasoning salt
4 tsp. soy sauce
2 Tbs. CHICKEN STYLE SEASONING
1 tsp. summer savory
1 tsp. marjoram

Mix seasonings and oil together and pour over the cereals and pretzels. Bake 2 hours at 200°. Put into hot jars to seal.

FROZEN GRAPES

Wash grapes. Drain. Line cookie sheet with wax paper. Put grapes on cookie sheet. Sprinkle with sugar, optional. Freeze. Take out and bag quickly. Store in freezer.

TRAIL MIX

raisins
date pieces
papaya
pineapple
apricots
cherries
apples
almonds
peanuts
cashews
walnuts
sunflower seeds
pumpkin seeds
carob chips

Make a mixture of your favorite dried fruits, nuts and seeds.

BAGELS see page 226

THIS SPACE FOR YOUR NOTES & RECIPES

_____

_____

_____

_____

_____

_____

_____

_____

_____

_____

_____

_____

_____

_____

_____

_____

THIS SPACE FOR YOUR NOTES & RECIPES

Menus & Recipes

Ice Box

Incidentals

THIS SPACE FOR YOUR NOTES & RECIPES

ALMOND MILK

1 c. almonds
2 c. water, No. 1
1/2 c. almonds, blanched
1/2 c. water, No. 2
2 1/2 c. water, No. 3
1/8 tsp. salt
1 tsp. vanilla
2 Tbs. honey or 1 chopped ring dried pineapple

Bring water No. 1 to a full boil. Immediately add almonds and let sit for 1 minute. Rinse under cold water and remove skins. Blend 1/2 c. almonds in the 1/2 c. water until smooth. Add remaining ingredients. May strain through cheese cloth. May repeat using the other half cup of nuts for another recipe of milk. Excellent on breakfast cereal.

PEAR MILK

1/3-1/2 c. almonds or cashews
1 c. water
1/4 tsp. vanilla
1/8 tsp. salt
1 Tbs. honey
canned pears
juice of pears

Blend all ingredients except pears until creamy. Add enough canned pears and juice, depending on how thick you want it, to make a quart of milk.

MILLET MILK

2/3 c. hot cooked millet
1/4-1/2 c. cashews
1 tsp. vanilla
1 tsp. salt
1 Tbs. honey
3 c. water

See page 41 for how to cook millet. Blend smooth all but 1 3/4 c. water. When smooth, add remaining water. Chill.

PEAR CREAM #1

1 c. cashews or blanched almonds
1/4 tsp. salt
1 tsp. vanilla
1-2 Tbs. honey
4 c. canned pears

Place first four ingredients into blender. Drain pears. Add juice to blender and blend smooth. Slowly add pears until thick. Chill and serve.

PEAR CREAM #2

1 qt. canned pears
juice of pears
4-6 Tbs. Tofu or Soy Milk powder
1/2 tsp. vanilla

Blend together in blender.

COCONUT CREAM

2 c. water
2/3 c. coconut
1/4 c. cornstarch
2 Tbs. honey, or more
1/4 tsp. salt

Blend coconut and water for 1 minute. Add remaining ingredients and continue to blend. Stir over medium heat until thickened. Chill and serve.

MILLET SAUCE

4 c. hot cooked MILLET
2 c. pineapple juice
1/2 banana
1 Tbs. vanilla
1/3 c. honey, or more

See page 41 for how to cook millet. Do not pack millet when measuring. Mix all ingredients. Blend smooth about 1/3 of the ingredients at a time. If the millet is hot it will blend more smoothly. Serve warm or chill. Chilling makes it thicker.

CREAM TOPPING

1 c. cooked rice or MILLET, hot
1/3 c. cashews
1 tsp. vanilla
1/4 c. chopped dates or 3 Tbs. honey
1/4 tsp. salt
1-1 1/2 c. water or MILK

See page 41 for how to cook millet. Blend all ingredients until creamy adding just enough water or milk to blend smooth. Chill.

STRAWBERRY YOGURT

1 1/2 c. cold water
1/2 c. cashews
1/2 c. hot cooked rice or MILLET
1 c. frozen strawberries
1/4 c. soft dates
1/8 tsp. salt
1 tsp. lemon juice

See page 41 for how to cook millet. Whiz cashews and rice in 1 c. water until smooth. Add remaining ingredients to blender. Chill and serve. May use other frozen fruit.

BLUEBERRY ORANGE SAUCE

2 c. water
3 Tbs. arrowroot
3/4 c. or 6 oz. frozen orange juice concentrate
1/4 c. honey
2-3 c. blueberries

Combine water and arrowroot. Bring to boil stirring constantly. Add honey. Remove from heat and add blueberries and orange juice. Cool and serve.

STRAWBERRIES & CRUSHED PINEAPPLE

4 c. partially thawed strawberries
2/3 c. water
2 Tbs. arrowroot powder or cornstarch
1 c. crushed pineapple
honey, optional

Drain juice from berries. Place juice in saucepan with starch and water. Bring to boil, stirring until thickened. Add remaining ingredients. Serve hot or cold.

MAPLE SYRUP

1 c. water
1 Tbs. arrowroot
1 c. honey
1 tsp. maple flavoring

Mix arrowroot and a little water into a paste. Add remaining water. Cook, stirring constantly, until clear and thick. Stir in honey and maple flavoring.

ORANGE DATE SYRUP

1 c. boiling water
1 c. pitted dates
3/4 c. frozen orange juice concentrate

Simmer water and dates together until soft. Remove from heat and add orange juice concentrate. Whiz in blender, pour into container and refrigerate.

APPLE SYRUP

2 c. apple juice or apple juice concentrate
2 Tbs. cornstarch or arrowroot powder
1/2 tsp. lemon juice
1/4 tsp. coriander, optional
1/8 tsp. cardamon, optional

Mix ingredients together and cook over medium heat until slightly thickened. Use on waffles or crepes, or as a glaze for sweet rolls.

BASIC NUT CREAM
(To replace shortening in recipes.)

3/4 c. nuts
1/2-1 1/4 c. water

Blend adding just enough water to make desired consistency, more for sauce and very little for butter. Blend until smooth. Salt may be added. Vanilla may be added for dessert recipes.

Note: When blending coconut, make sure you blend very fine, until it turns greasy.

CORN BUTTER

2 tsp. Emes unflavored gelatin
1/4 c. cold water
1 c. boiling water
1 c. unsalted, hot, corn meal mush
1/4 c. cashews
1 1/2 tsp. salt
2 tsp. lemon juice
enough grated raw carrot for color

Soak gelatin in the cold water for a few minutes in blender while assembling other ingredients. Pour the 1 cup of boiling water over gelatin, and whiz to dissolve. Add remaining ingredients and blend thoroughly until smooth as cream. Cool and refrigerate.

GARLIC BUTTER

1 c. water
3/4 c. hot cornmeal mush
1/2 c. raw cashews
2-4 garlic cloves
1 Tbs. yeast flakes
1 Tbs. onion flakes
1 tsp. salt
4 tsp. lemon juice
1/2 c. sesame seeds
1/2 tsp. marjoram, optional
1/2 tsp. dill weed, optional

Liquefy all but the last three ingredients until smooth, about 2 minutes. Briefly whiz in sesame seeds and herbs. Yields 2 1/2 c. Spread thickly on bread slices and broil until crusty and beginning to brown.

GRAPE JAM

4 c. grape juice
2 c. washed currants
1/4 c. Minute tapioca

Mix all ingredients. Let sit 15 minutes or longer. Bring to boil over medium heat stirring constantly. Cook until tapioca is clear. Chill and serve. May choose to blend after cooking to make jam more smooth.

TROPICAL FRUIT SPREAD

2/3 part dried pineapple
1/3 part dried papaya
pineapple or orange juice

Cover dried fruit with juice and let stand overnight. Drain and put fruit in blender adding enough juice until it blends smooth. Chill and serve. A quicker way to make the spread is to mix equal amounts of dried fruit and juice. Bring to a boil. Lightly boil 5 minutes. Remove from heat. Let sit 5 minutes then blend ingredients until smooth.

GRANDMA'S OLD FASHIONED RASPBERRY JAM

Method #1 - Using no sugar
3 c. raspberries, fresh or frozen
5 rings dried pineapple
Pineapple or orange juice as needed for consistency

Rinse dried pineapple in water to remove any sulphur. Cut dried pineapple into small pieces. Combine all ingredients and let sit until pineapple is soft. If using frozen fruit, do night before. Set pineapple in bottom of bowl and put frozen fruit on top of pineapple. Stir and then blend until smooth. Add juice if necessary.

Method #2 - Using 1/2 the normal amount of sugar generally used in jam recipes.

6 c. raspberries, fresh or frozen
1 Tbs. lemon juice
Let boil 2 minutes then add:
3 c. sugar

Bring to rolling boil and boil 3 minutes. Remove from heat and whip with beater 5 minutes. If canning, put into jars using open kettle method.

STRAWBERRY JAM

2 c. fresh or frozen strawberries
4-5 rings of dried pineapple
pineapple or orange juice as needed for consistency

Rinse dried pineapple in water to remove any sulphur. Cut dried pineapple into small pieces. Combine all ingredients and let set until diced pineapple is soft. Blend in blender until smooth. It may not need any juice if the strawberries have enough liquid.

CERA JEL JAMS

4 c. canned fruit or mixture of fruits: pears, peaches, apricots
1/4 c. soaked raisins
1/4 c. soaked dates, pitted
1-2 Tbs. cera jel powder

Blend the above together adding jel last in order to get the right amount to thicken the fruit. The hole in the center, while blending, will slowly close. May use the imagination and add dried soaked fruit of your choice, currants, pineapple and etc.
Variation: 1-2 rings dried pineapple may be used in place of dates and raisins.
Cera Jel is pre-cooked "food starch-modified" derived from waxy corn. It thickens immediately upon contact with liquid thus blending is the easiest way to get it mixed in evenly, or sprinkling with a shaker and stirring quickly as it is sprinkled. Bakers combine it with sugar to prevent lumping. It is very convenient for non-cooking thickening. Purchase at a bakery supply.

APRICOT JAM

4 quarts apricots, pitted and cut
3 c. pineapple, crushed or tidbit
1 c. raisins
1 c. currants or more raisins
1 c. chopped dates
3/4 c. orange juice concentrate
honey to taste

Bring first five ingredients to slow boil and simmer until soft. May choose to blend smooth. Add the orange juice and sweeten to taste. Fill into hot jars and process for 20 minutes in a hot water bath.

CHERRY RASPBERRY JAM

6 c. cherries, fresh or frozen
2 1/2 - 3 c. dried pineapple, diced
2 c. fresh or frozen thawed raspberries
1 tsp. lemon juice
2-3 tsp. agar powder

Mash cherries and soak pineapple until soft. Blend or whiz. Bring to boil and boil 10 minutes then add raspberries, lemon juice and agar powder. Boil another 5 minutes. Whip with beater 5 minutes.

DRIED FRUIT JAM

1 c. dried fruit: prunes, cherries, pears, apricots, etc.
water enough to cover fruit
honey, if needed

Cook over medium heat until fruit is soft. Blend in blender with liquid that was used to cook fruit; amount depending on your desired consistency for the jam. Add honey while blending.

PINEAPPLE PRUNE JAM

1 1/4 c. packed prunes
1 c. pineapple juice
1 1/2 c. crushed pineapple, drained
1 c. packed, pitted dates
3/4 c.or 6 oz. frozen orange juice concentrate
1/2 tsp. lemon extract

Soak prunes in 1 c. water few hours or lightly boil in water a few minutes, until soft. Drain. Bring dates and pineapple juice to a boil. Put in blender with remaining ingredients, except crushed pineapple. Blend, leaving mixture somewhat chunky. Stir in pineapple.

NUT RAISIN SPREAD

1 c. cashews
1 c. almonds
1 Tbs. grated lemon peel
1/2 tsp. ground coriander
1 c. orange juice
1 c. raisins

Place nuts in food processor. Grind to a paste. Stir in remaining ingredients. May add all ingredients to food processor after grinding nuts. Makes 36 - 1 Tbs. servings.

APPLE BUTTER

2 apples
1/2 c. pitted dates
1/2 c. water

Wash and core apples. Dice and cook with dates and water until apples are tender. Blend until smooth.

MAYONNAISE & DRESSING

TOFU MAYONNAISE

1/3 c. nuts, blanched almonds or cashews
1/3 c. water
1/4 c. lemon juice
1 lb. tofu
1 tsp. salt
1 tsp. onion powder
1 Tbs. honey

Blend all ingredients until smooth. Chill and serve. Keeps in refrigerator for a week.

AVOCADO DRESSING

Blend:1/3 c. TOFU MAYONNAISE
1 large avocado

Add enough cold water to make desired consistency. Chill. Add extra seasoning if desired such as onion or garlic powder.

ALMOND-POTATO MAYONNAISE

1/2 c. blanched almonds
1 - 1 1/2 c. water
1 tsp. honey
1/2 - 1 tsp. salt
2 Tbs. lemon juice, or to taste
1/2 - 1 cooked potato
Optional: dill, garlic, sweet basil, etc.

Blend smooth 1 c. water and nuts. Add remaining ingredients. While blending add enough cooked potato to make thick consistency.

SOY CASHEW MAYONNAISE

1 c. cold water
1/2 tsp. salt
1/8 tsp. garlic powder
1/2 c. cashews
1/2 tsp. onion powder
1/3 c. soy milk powder
1/3 c. oil
2-4 Tbs. lemon juice

Blend first six ingredients. While blending, very slowly add oil. Stop blender and add lemon juice. Stir with a spoon to mix. Chill and serve.

JAN'S MAYONNAISE

1/2 c. cashews
1/2 c. SOY BASE, see recipe below
2 Tbs. lemon juice
1 1/2 tsp. salt
1 tsp. onion powder
1/8 tsp. garlic powder
2 1/4 c. water
2-3 Tbs. Cera Jel

Blend smooth all ingredients except 1 c. water and Cera Jel. When smooth, add remaining water. Add Cera Jel at the end, thickening to desired thickness.

SOY BASE

1 c. soy flour
2 c. water

Blend or stir water and soy flour together. Use one of the following methods to cook: 1) Cook in a double boiler for a couple hours until it thickens. Stir occasionally. 2) Cook in crock pot on high, covered, for 3-4 hours. Stir occasionally. 3) Place simmer ring on burner. Place covered saucepan on ring. Lightly boil about 30 minutes, stirring occasionally. 4) Place ingredients in a covered casserole dish. Bake at 350° for 60 minutes. Stir occasionally.
Helpful hint: Make a large quantity at one time. When cool, place in cup or 1/2 cup size portions on a cookie sheet and freeze. When frozen, put in a plastic bag, and put back in freezer. You now have soy base ready for future use for any recipe that calls for it.

SOY MAYONNAISE

1 c. water
1/2 c. Soyagen
1/2 tsp. salt
1/2 tsp. paprika
1/4 tsp. garlic powder
1/4 tsp. onion powder
1-3 Tbs. lemon juice
cooked potato or hot cooked rice

Whiz together slowly. Slowly add cooked potatoes or rice until thick. Whiz 1 minute. Remove and stir in lemon juice. Refrigerate.

SESAME DRESSING

1 1/3 c. water
1/2 c. sesame seeds, ground dry in blender
2 tsp. honey
1 1/2 tsp. salt
1 Tbs. onion, fresh
1/4 tsp. garlic, fresh
1 tsp. lemon powder or 2 Tbs. lemon juice

Blend smooth all ingredients with 1/2 c. water. Add remaining water.

FRENCH DRESSING

2 c. tomatoes, canned
1/4 tsp. Italian seasoning
1 tsp. CHICKEN STYLE SEASONING or 1/2 tsp. salt + 1/4 tsp.
   basil
1/2 tsp. onion powder
1/2 tsp. garlic powder
1 Tbs. honey
2 Tbs. lemon juice
salt to taste

Blend well.

Variation: Add 1 c. cashew milk. Make this by blending smooth 1/2 c. cashews, 3/4 c. water, 1/8 tsp. salt.

THOUSAND ISLAND DRESSING

1/3 c. tomato juice
1/3 c. blanched almonds or cashews
3 Tbs. lemon juice
1/2 c. tomato juice
1 1/2 tsp. honey
1 tsp. salt
1 Tbs. onion powder
1/2 tsp. paprika
1 c. firm tofu
parsley

Blend smooth first three ingredients. Add remaining ingredients except tofu. Gradually add approximately 1 c. firm tofu to make desired consistency. Pour into bowl and stir in 1 Tbs. dried or 2 Tbs. fresh parsley. Then add to your own taste: minced olives, raw onion and pimento.

TROPICAL DRESSING

1 c. SOY MAYONNAISE
1 mashed banana
1/2 c. crushed pineapple
1/4 c. coconut

Leave out onion and garlic powder and paprika out of mayonnaise. Mix all ingredients. Use on any kind of fruit salad.

PEAR CREAM

1 c. cashews or blanched almonds
1/4 tsp. salt
1 tsp. vanilla
1-2 Tbs. honey
4 c. canned pears

Place first four ingredients into blender. Drain pears. Add juice to blender and blend smooth. Slowly add pears until thick. Chill and serve.

HINT FOR MAKING CHEESE
Freeze your red peppers or pimentos in peak season. Use as needed.

PIMENTO CHEESE SAUCE

1 c. water
1 c. cashews
1 tsp. salt
1/4 tsp. ground dill seed
1/8 tsp. garlic powder
3 Tbs. nutritional yeast flakes
1/2 c. pimento, 4 oz. jar
1/4 c. lemon juice

Blend smooth all ingredients.
Variation: Leave out 1/2 c. cashews. After blending, bring ingredients to a light boil. stirring, for about 3 minutes. It will thicken. Chilling the cooked sauce will make it thicker.

GARBANZO-PIMENTO CHEESE

2 c. soaked garbanzo beans
1/3 c. brazil nuts
1/4 c. nutritional yeast flakes
1/2 c. or 4 oz. pimentos or red pepper
1/2 tsp. onion powder
1/8 tsp. garlic powder
1/4 c. lemon juice
1-1 1/2 c. water
1 tsp. salt

Soak 1 c. beans in 3 c. water at least 6 hours. Drain. Blend garbanzos with enough of the water in the recipe to blend smooth. Add remaining ingredients to blender and blend smooth. Place in double boiler and cook 25-30 minutes, stirring occasionally. Pour into greased mold and chill. Unmold, slice and serve.

JACK CHEESE

1/2 c. water
1/4 c. Emes unflavored gelatin
3/4 c. boiling water
1 c. cashews
1/4 c. nutritional yeast flakes
1 1/2 tsp. salt
1 tsp. onion powder
1/4 tsp. garlic powder
1/4 c. lemon juice
1/4 c. finely grated carrot or red pepper for color

Soak gelatin in the 1/2 c. water in blender, while assembling remaining ingredients. Pour boiling water over soaked gelatin and whiz briefly to dissolve. Cool slightly. Add cashews and liquefy thoroughly. Add remaining ingredients. Liquefy until mixture is creamy. Pour into container, cool slightly. Cover and refrigerate overnight before using. Slice and serve.

PARMESAN CHEESE

1 c. nutritional yeast flakes
1 c. sunflower seeds, ground dry in blender
2 tsp. garlic powder
2 tsp. onion powder
4 tsp. CHICKEN STYLE SEASONING
2 Tbs. lemon juice

Mix first 2 ingredients together adding seasonings. Add lemon juice mixing well. Put into tightly sealed jars. Keeps well. Use in pizza, haystacks and tacos.

COTTAGE CHEESE

1 lb. tofu
1/4 tsp. garlic powder
1/4 tsp. onion powder
1/2 tsp. lemon juice
1 tsp. salt
1/2 c. cashews

Rinse and crumble tofu. Blend remaining ingredients. Add enough pickle juice or water to make creamy. If using pickle juice, reduce salt. Mix cream with crumbled tofu. Chill and serve.

DEBBIE'S GRATING CHEESE

1/2 c. water
3 Tbs. Emes unflavored gelatin
3/4 c. hot cooked millet
1/4 c. cashews
1 Tbs. lemon juice, fresh is best
1 tsp. salt
1 1/2 tsp. onion powder
2 Tbs. yeast flakes
pimento for color
1 1/2 tsp. dill weed

Soak water and gelatin in blender for 5 minutes. Blend briefly. Add remaining ingredients. Blend well. Spray the inside of an empty 16 oz. can with a nonstick spray such as "Pam". Pour blended ingredients into the can. Put into refrigerator. Cut out other side of the can and slide out. Grate over favorite dishes. Especially good over enchiladas and pizza.

VELVEETA CHEESE

1/3 c. Emes unflavored gelatin
1 c. water
3/4 c. sesame seeds ground dry in blender
1/3 c. lemon juice
1 c. water
1/2 c. canned pimento or red pepper
1 lb. tofu
1/4 c. yeast flakes
1 Tbs. onion powder
1/2 tsp. garlic powder
2 1/2 tsp. salt
2 c. cornmeal mush, unsalted

Bring water to boil and stir in gelatin. Blend smooth next 5 ingredients. Empty into bowl. Blend smooth remaining ingredients with gelatin water. Mix together all ingredients. Put in greased container and refrigerate until firm. Turn out and slice.

MELTY CHEESE

2 c. water
1/2 c. or 4 oz. pimento, canned
1/4 c. yeast flakes
1 1/2 tsp. salt
1/2 tsp. onion powder
1/4 tsp. garlic powder
3 Tbs. cornstarch
1/4 c. cashews or almonds
1-2 Tbs. lemon juice

Blend smooth 1 c. of the water with the remaining ingredients. Add remaining water and blend. Cook until thick, 5-6 minutes, stirring constantly. Great for dip for chips or as sauce. Can be frozen.

SOY CREAM CHEESE

2 Tbs. Emes unflavored gelatin
1/3 c. water
1/2 c. boiling water
1 c. cashews
1-2 tsp. salt, according to taste
2 Tbs. lemon juice
1 1/2 lb. tofu

Soak gelatin in 1/3 cup water in blender for a few minutes. Add 1/2 cup boiling water and whiz briefly to dissolve. Add remaining ingredients. Liquefy well. Place in rectangular mold and refrigerate until set.

PIMENTO CREAM CHEESE

2-3 c. SOY CREAM CHEESE
2-3 pimentos or 1 1/2 red peppers
2 Tbs. yeast flakes
2 tsp. onion powder
1/2 tsp. garlic powder

Almost liquefy pimentos, leaving some small flecks. Add pimentos and remaining seasonings to Soy Cream Cheese.

SOY CREAM CHEESE WITH CHIVES

Stir 1/4 cup minced chives into 2 cups SOY CREAM CHEESE.

CREAM CHEESE WITH OLIVES

Stir 1 cup chopped black olives into 2 cups SOY CREAM CHEESE.

HERBED CREAM CHEESE BALLS

Stir 1 tsp. herb of your choice into 2 cups SOY CREAM CHEESE. Form into small balls and roll in finely minced parsley.

BONANZA BEAN DIP

2 Tbs. olive oil
1/3 c. lemon juice, or more
1/2 clove garlic
1/2 tsp. garlic salt or salt to taste
Pinch ground cumin or other herbs to taste
2 c. cooked white or pinto beans, drained

Mash all together. Serve at room temperature.

MARY'S BROWN GRAVY

1/2 c. almonds or cashews
1 c. water
2 c. water
1/4 c. whole wheat flour
1/8 tsp. garlic salt
1 tsp. salt
1 tsp. CHICKEN STYLE SEASONING or 1/4 tsp. salt
beef style seasoning
1 tsp. soy sauce
1 tsp. marmite or 1 1/2 Tbs. soy sauce

Blend almonds and water until smooth. Add remaining ingredients. Blend well, cook and bring to boil, stirring constantly. If too thick add more water. Makes 3 cups.

ONION GRAVY

1 c. finely chopped onion
1 c. finely chopped celery
1/2 c. almonds or other nuts
1 c. water
1/3 c. white flour
2 tsp. CHICKEN STYLE SEASONING
1 tsp. salt
2 c. water

Saute onion and celery. Blend almonds and 1 c.water. Add remaining ingredients. Blend well and add to celery and onions and stirring constantly bring to boil. If too thick, add more water. Makes 1 1/2 quarts.

CASHEW GRAVY

1 c. cashews
5 c. water
1/4 c. flour
1 1/2 Tbs. marmite or 1/4 c. soy sauce
2 tsp. onion powder
1/4 tsp. garlic powder
1/2-1 tsp. salt

Blend smooth all ingredients with 1 1/2 c. of the water. Add remaining water. Lightly boil, stirring, until thickened.

ALMOND GRAVY

2 c. water
1/2 c. almonds, ground dry in blender
2 Tbs. arrowroot
2 tsp. onion powder
1/2-1 tsp. salt

Blend all ingredients well. Lightly boil, stirring, until thickened, about 3 minutes. May add fresh chopped parsley if desired.

CANNING

For a few years I tried to can without any sugar and after all that work the fruit would just sit there or my husband's stomach would burn from the unpalatable fruit. So after thinking and praying I have incorporated this thought, "It is especially necessary that the fruit for canning should be in good condition. Use little sugar, and cook the fruit only long enough to ensure its preservation. Thus prepared, it is an excellent substitute for fresh fruit." Ministry of Healing, page 299. My family is much happier now. The canned fruit is so much nicer. One does not have to use much sugar to keep it preserved nicely and to bring out the delectable flavors of the different fruits. A few tablespoons of sugar or honey for the sweeter tree ripened fruits is all you need. I have found for PRUNES that freezing them and then cooking them in their own juices and adding only enough sweetener to taste is par to none. The flavor is so nice! Otherwise the open kettle method for canning prunes would be the same idea.

Using fruit juice to replace sugar is another method, though it sometimes can be a bit more costly. The juice prevents the water from pulling out the sugar (flavor) from the fruit. The tarter fruits such as APRICOTS need sugar along with the juice. One part water to two parts apple juice is a good starter. Best to test for your own family's taste. Apple juice seems to blend in with the flavor of the fruit you are canning. So for example:

APPLESAUCE

Golden Delicious apples make sweet applesauce with half water and half apple juice. Make adjustments to suit your taste when using other apples.

PEACHES

2 c. apple juice, 1 c. water

RASPBERRIES

2 c. apple juice, 1 c. water. Berries often require undiluted apple juice.

BLUEBERRIES

2 c. apple juice, 1 c. water

CHERRIES

2 c. apple juice, 1 c. water

PEARS

2 c. apple juice, 1 c. water

PRUNES, see paragraph at the top of this page.
APRICOTS, see paragraph at the top of this page.

METHOD

1. Prepare fruit as for any canning by washing and paring if desired.
2. Mix fruit juice. Juice may be used hot or cold depending upon how quickly it will be canned.
3. Pour one cup of juice into each jar before filling. This prevents problems with bubbles.
4. Place fruit in jar within 1/2 inch from top. Fill with juice.
5. Place sealer and ring and screw tight.
6. Place in canner, cover one quart jars with water and bring to gentle boil for 20 minutes. This applies to all fruit.
7. Do not allow hard boiling or liquid will boil out of jar and often preventing sealing.
8. Remove canner from heat and allow to cool 5 minutes before removing jars from canner. Remove jars one at a time and place on a towel to cool.

DILL PICKLES

2 1/2 c. lemon juice
1 1/2 qts. water
16 grape leaves
8 cloves garlic
1/3 c. course pickling salt
16 stalks of dill or 1/4 c. dill seed
8 qts. small cucumbers

Place grape leaf and part of dill in bottom of jar. Pack cucumbers into jar. Put rest of dill on top. Bring to a boil the lemon juice, water and salt. Pour brine into jar to within 1/2 inch from top. Cover with grape leaf. Seal with hot, boiled lids. Boil in hot water bath for 5 minutes.

CRUNCHY DILL PICKLES

Brine:
4 qts. water
2 c. lemon juice
3/4 c. pickling salt
fresh dill
garlic, optional

Pack jars alternately with firm cucumbers and sprigs of fresh dill. Bring water, lemon juice and salt to full boil. Pour boiling brine over cucumbers in jars and immediately screw on hot boiled lids. Do not process any further, but put the sealed jars where they can be watched for two weeks to make sure they stay sealed. If they do unseal, use right away. Any size jar may be used, and do not pack the jars too tightly.

PICKLED BEETS

Cooked beets
1/4-1/3 c. lemon juice
1 Tbs. sugar
1/2 tsp. salt

Cook beets until skins slip off easily. Slice into quart jars and add the measurement of lemon juice, sugar and salt to each jar. Fill remainder of jar with water up to 1/2 inch from the top. Process in water bath for 30 minutes.

BREAD AND BUTTER PICKLES OR RELISH

2 Tbs. celery seed
2 c. brown sugar
2 c. lemon juice
2 c. water
2 tsp. turmeric
4 qts. large cucumbers
8 onions
2 red peppers
2 green peppers
1/4 c. pickling salt

Slice cucumbers, onions, peppers. Layer with table salt and let set for 3 hours, then drain. Combine remaining ingredients and bring to boil. Fill hot jars quickly. Let seal.Variation: Can be ground into a relish, omit 2 c. of water.

LOW-CAL MUSTARD

1 clove garlic
1/3 c. lemon juice
1/2 c. water
1-2 Tbs. oil
1 tsp. tumeric
1/2 tsp. salt
1/4 c. flour

Put last 5 ingredients in blender to mix. Put in sauce pan and cook until thickened. Return to blender and add garlic. While blending, slowly add the lemon juice. Refrigerate to chill and thicken.

KETCHUP

6 oz. can tomato paste
1 Tbs. honey
1 tsp. salt
3 Tbs. lemon juice
1/4 tsp. garlic powder
1/4 tsp. onion powder

Tomatoes, tomato juice or water enough to make the mixture blend smooth.

CRANBERRY SAUCE

1 package cranberries
1 large apple
1/2 orange, including peeling
1/2 - 1/3 c. honey

If possible, freeze cranberries first. Blend a few at a time in blender, so they don't mush. Grate apple. Blend orange including peel or just use orange juice. If you do not have a blender, chop like you would parsley. Add melted honey.

STEWED PRUNES

Pit and freeze plums. When ready to use, heat in kettle with small amount of water. Bring to boil, simmer until nicely stewed. Add desired amount of honey. May use frozen grape juice concentrate in place of water and honey.

ORANGE RIND

Cut up orange peeling from six oranges in strips. Cover with water and add 2-3 tsp. salt. Boil 10 minutes. Rinse and add fresh water and boil until orange rind is soft. Drain and put enough honey to make a glaze, 1/2-3/4 c. honey. Simmer until clear and thick. Mash with fork and use in favorite recipes. Store in refrigerator.

SOY SAUCE

20 raw black beans
1/2 onion
1/2 carrot, chopped
10 mushrooms
1-2 broccoli stems with flowers or heads
1 c. water or vegetable broth
1 tsp. salt

Lightly boil all ingredients until water turns black. Drain in sieve. Discard pulp. Refrigerate or freeze. NOTE: Alternate seasoning to Soy Sauce are Maggi, Bragg Liquid Aminos, Dr. Bronner's Bouillon, Aroma, or Knorr Liquid Seasoning found in some supermarkets, healthfood stores, food coops, bulk food stores.

JAR METHOD OF GROWING SPROUTS

1. Soak 3 Tbs. alfalfa seeds in quart jar overnight. Attach hardware cloth or nylon stocking to top of jar.
2. Drain water and rinse seeds well.
3. Turn jar upside down in bowl or wire stand and put in a dark, warm place, such as a cupboard.
4. Rinse seeds through screen twice each day, 3 times in the summer. Keep jar inverted. Gently shake seeds evenly to distribute around well of jar.
5. Most sprouts are ready to use when they are 1/4 in. to 1/2 in. long. Alfalfa sprouts are best a little longer. After 2 days, put in sun to develop bright green color (Vitamin A and Chlorophyll).

CURRY POWDER

1 1/2 Tbs. garlic powder
2 Tbs. turmeric
2 Tbs. coriander, ground
2 Tbs. cumin, ground

Mix together and use as needed.

JAN'S VEGETABLE SEASONING MIX

2 c. dried vegetable flakes
1/3 c. CHICKEN STYLE SEASONING
6 Tbs. salt
2 Tbs. onion powder
2 tsp. celery salt
2 tsp. garlic powder
1 tsp. paprika

Grind vegetable flakes to powder in blender. Then mix in a bowl all ingredients. Store in a covered jar for future use. Use 1 tsp. per cup of liquid. Put any herbs or seasoning in of your choice. Use as an alternate seasoning for Ramen Noodles and other dishes of your choice.

CHICKEN STYLE SEASONING

1 1/3 c. yeast flakes
3 Tbs. onion powder
2 1/2 tsp. garlic powder
1 Tbs. salt
1 tsp. celery seed
2 1/2 Tbs. Italian seasoning
2 Tbs. parsley, dried

Blend smooth all except parsley. Stir in parsley. Seal in airtight container.

THIS SPACE FOR YOUR NOTES & RECIPES

Menus & Recipes

Pantry Basics

THIS SPACE FOR YOUR NOTES & RECIPES

BREADS

"Wherefore do ye spend money for that which is not bread? And your labour for that which satisfieth not?" Isa. 55:2. Are you spending money for that which is not bread? Are you buying fluffy white bread like 97% of the rest of our nation? Even during the war years when nutritious foods were hard to come by, it was not possible to stop the love affair between North Americans and white flour products. The government decided to settle for a second best situation called enrichment. Even though the word enriched gives the idea of getting riches, the following story may reveal loss rather than gain.

Three groups of chickens were fed diets as follows:
Group A - 100% whole wheat flour
Group B - Enriched white flour
Group C - Unenriched white flour

The results of these diets for the rapidly growing chicks were as follows: Group C all died within five days due to the lack of nutrients found in unenriched white flour.

Group B feathered out but appeared more nervous and jittery with a high pitched chirp. They ran in and our through their food and water dishes making flour boots for their feet.

Group A feathered out and gained weight in a normal fashion. They did not display the nervousness of those raised on the enriched white flour.

We can conclude that plumpness and condition of skin, hair or feathers are not the only criteria to be used to determine the adequacy of a diet. Cheerfulness, self-control, mental efficiency and productivity all count in this determination.

The problem of enrichment is out weighted by a more crucial difficulty in refinement. Even the enriched flour lacks the bran or outer protective coating of the wheat kernel. The bran in indigestible fiber which absorbs water in the digestive tract and provides bulk and stimulates the normal movements necessary to the bowel. According to Dr. Burkett our diet promotes constipation because of a lack of these indigestible fibers found in bran, with resulting digestive track diseases like diverticular disease, hemorrhoids, colon cancer and appendicitis. He goes so far as to say England and America are totally constipated nations with a three-day to two-weeks transit time-the time in comparison to a rural African population which has a 30-hour transit time, is the time it takes for the food to pass through the digestive track beginning to end. Whole grains are delicious and nutritious. Here are some breads that you will enjoy tasting and your body will enjoy digesting.

TIPS FOR SUCCESS IN BREADMAKING

Don't start a batch of bread until you have read the recipe all the way through. Know that you have the proper ingredients or suitable substitutes, and understand the mixing method.

If you are just learning to bake, try a simple basic recipe first.

Use only fresh, best quality flours. The high gluten content of hard wheat flour makes it best for breadmaking. A mixture of two or three flours is more nutritious than only one, as the elements of one will supplement the elements of the other.

Keep the temperature right. An off-flavor develops in bread that is allowed to get too warm. Too cool a temperature prolongs the rising. Yeast plants grow best at a temperature of 84 degrees.

Salt and fat both retard the growth of the yeast and should not be added to a yeast mixture until it has grown strong and lively, feeding on sugar and starch. Too much sugar also tends to retard the action of yeast somewhat.

Develop the gluten in the wheat flour by beating the batter thoroughly before adding other flours which have little or no gluten.

A poor job of kneading the dough before the first rising period cannot be remedied. A good way to knead is to lift the dough with the fingers, spread to support it from underneath, fold it over and push down hard with the heels of the hands. Do this over and over, counting the strokes. It usually takes 200 strokes.

When the dough is ready to mold into loaves, grease your hands and the pans, form the dough into a smooth ball or loaf, and tuck it in so that the edges touch the sides of the pan, snugly and smoothly.

Never fill pans too full; give the bread room to expand without having to billow out the edges, causing cracked, over-browned crusts. Pans should be about half full or a little more.

Always preheat the oven before the bread is ready to go in. It is a good idea to turn it on when you start molding the loaves, as this warms the kitchen and helps the bread to rise quickly.

When the bread is doubled in bulk and ready to bake, a slight indentation made with the finger will remain. It should be "a little on the green side" rather than over-raised.

The loaves should be small and thoroughly baked. No taint of yeast should be present in the bread when the loaf is out. Most 1 lb. loaves bake in 35-40 minutes. A larger, heavy loaf takes longer.

Don't cover baked bread with airtight material, such as a plastic bag while it is cooling unless you want a soft, slightly damp crust. Instead, cover bread with a towel as it cools.

"Just out of the oven" bread is difficult to digest. Bread should be at least 12 hours old before it is eaten.

Never let your baking become monotonous. Once you are familiar with the process of baking, use your imagination to experiment with different ingredients and combinations. Bread freezes well so don't be afraid to make up several different kinds at one time.

COMMON BREAD DEFECTS AND POSSIBLE CAUSES

SOUR YEASTY TASTE:
-Water too warm
-Insufficiently baked
-Period of rising too long, especially in whole grain breads which will not rise as light as white breads
-Temperature too high while rising
-Poor yeast

DRY OR CRUMBLY:
-Too much flour in dough
-Not enough kneading
-Over-baking
-Letting loaves rise too high before baking

HEAVINESS:
-Too much flour added
-Insufficient kneading
-Old flour
-Old yeast

CRACKS IN CRUST:
-Cooling in a draft
-Baking before sufficiently light
-Oven too hot at first

TOO THICK A CRUST:
-Oven too slow
-Bakes too long
-Excess salt

SOGGINESS:
-Too much liquid
-Insufficient baking
-Cooling in airtight container

ILL SHAPED LOAF:
-Not molded well originally
-Too large a loaf for the pan
-Rising period too long
-Failure to rise to greatest size in oven
-Loaves flat on top may result from inadequate kneading or using too much flour that is low in gluten such as rye, millet, rice, cornmeal, oat flour

COARSE GRAIN:
-Too much liquid
-Too high temperature during rising
-Rising too long or proofing too long
-Oven too cool at first
-Pan too large for size of loaf

JUNE'S WHOLE WHEAT BREAD

1/2 c. raisins
1 apple, cut in pieces
1 c. hot water
5 c. very warm water
2 c. rolled oats
5 c. whole wheat flour
2 Tbs. salt
2 Tbs. yeast
2 Tbs. gluten flour, optional
2 Tbs. liquid lecithin or granules, optional
1/2 tsp. vitamin C powder, optional

Blend first three ingredients together in blender. Pour blended mixture into a bread mixing bowl (Bosch). Then add remaining ingredients. Mix well together. Beat well, or knead well. Let sit for 10 minutes thus giving the flour time to absorb the liquid which means you will use less flour total. When making Raisin Bread at this point add raisins, chopped walnuts, fruit or anything you may wish to add to make either raisin bread or fruit bread. Then add, beat well or knead well, 8-10 more cups of whole wheat flour. Half of this could be unbleached white flour when you use this recipe for buns, or raisin bread. Knead or beat well for about 8-10 minutes to develop the gluten in the flour. Let rest for another 10 minutes. Shape into loaves or buns, put in pans. Let rise 30 minutes or until about doubled in bulk. Bake in a preheated oven at 350° for 45 minutes for bread, 30 minutes for buns. I only use optional items when I am having trouble with certain wheat or flour not rising well.

SPROUTED WHEAT BREAD - BREAD MIXER METHOD

12 c. wheat
1 c. raisins
1 c. hot apple juice
3 Tbs. yeast
1 1/2 Tbs. salt or less, to taste
1 c. gluten flour

Soak 12 cups wheat in about 6 quarts of water for 36-48 hours. In the summer use cool water and in the cold weather use warm water. Change water every 6-8 hours. Blend raisins and juice. Put soaked wheat through food grinder. Grind wheat into the bowl that you will be using to make your bread in. Then start adding your raisin mixture to the ground up wheat. Add yeast, salt and gluten flour. Add enough whole wheat flour to make a soft but firm dough. Mix well for about 10-15 minutes. Shape into loaves and put into, greased pans. Let rise for 30-40 minutes. Bake at 350° for 40-45 minutes.

Note: Use a 1/8 inch whole diameter disk in your meat grinder for grinding the wheat.

DARK RYE BREAD

4 c. warm water
2 Tbs. yeast
2 Tbs. lecithin
1/3 c. pure sorghum or molasses
1 c. raw grated potato or 1/2 c. mashed
1/4 c. soy sauce
2 tsp. salt, heaping
2 Tbs. ground caraway seed
4 c. rye flour
5 c. whole wheat flour or part oat
4 3/4 c. unbleached white flour
1/4 c. soy flour

Mix first four ingredients together. Let set 10 minutes. Add next four ingredients mixing well. Add remaining ingredients. Knead bread well using the last 3/4 c. of unbleached flour as you are kneading. Add just enough flour to make a soft but not sticky dough. Let rise until double in warm place. Shape into five loaves. Let rise in pans until double. Bake at 350° for 55-60 minutes or until done depending on size of loaves. May be shaped into rye buns or rolls of many different shapes. Bake rolls or buns for about 25-35 minutes depending on their size.

RYE BREAD

4 c. boiling water
3/4 c. molasses
1 Tbs. salt
2 Tbs. caraway seeds
1/4 c. honey
2 c. rye flour
1 c. warm water
2 Tbs. yeast
1 Tbs. brown sugar
11-13 c. mixture of whole wheat and unbleached white flour

Mix first six ingredients together and let cool to lukewarm. Dissolve next three ingredients together and add to molasses mixture. Stir in whole wheat flour and unbleached white flour until you have a reasonably soft dough to knead. Knead 5-10 minutes. Let rise and then form into five round loaves. Place on 2 oiled cookie sheets. Let rise until double. Bake at 350° for 50-60 minutes.

WHOLE WHEAT CARROT BREAD

1 Tbs. yeast
1/4 c. warm water
2 tsp. honey
1 1/2 c. warm water
1/4 c. molasses
2 Tbs. gluten flour, optional
2 medium carrots
1 c. hot tap water
2 Tbs. liquid lecithin, optional
2 1/2 tsp. salt
8-9 c. whole wheat flour

Add yeast and honey to water and let soften about 10 minutes. Combine next three ingredients with yeast mixture. Beat until well mixed. Let rise until bubbly-about 30 minutes. Whiz carrots and lecithin with water in blender or grate fine and combine with water. Add to yeast sponge. Add flour and salt, making a very stiff dough. Knead on a well floured board for 10 minutes. Place in oiled bowl, turning dough over. Cover and let rise until double in bulk. Punch down. Let rise until double again. Shape into loaves. Let rise until double. Bake at 350° for 45 minutes.

HOSKA BRAIDED BREAD

6 c. water
1/3 c. honey
3 Tbs. yeast
1/4 c. lecithin
1/4 c. lemon juice
3 c. unbleached white flour
3 c. whole wheat flour
1 1/2 Tbs. salt
3 c. unbleached white flour
3 c. whole wheat flour
2 c. raisins
1 c. almonds, chopped

Mix first seven ingredients together and let sit 10 minutes. Add remaining ingredients. Knead and add enough flour to make soft-not sticky dough. Let rise two times. Divide into sections to be braided. Make two layers of braid. Top shorter than bottom. Hold into place with toothpicks. Let rise. Bake 15 minutes at 375° and then 20 minutes at 350°. Remove toothpicks and decorate when cool.

BREAD STICKS

2 c. warm water
2 Tbs. brown sugar
2 tsp. salt
1 1/2 tsp. onion powder
2 Tbs. yeast
1/2 c. ground nuts
5 c. flour

Mix first four ingredients together and then stir in yeast and nuts. Mix in flour. Beat vigorously. Don't knead. Cover and refrigerate overnight. Roll into rolls or sticks. Put on oiled cookie sheet. Let rise in warm place until almost double in size. Bake 12-15 minutes at 400°.

VARIATIONS FOR USE OF BREAD DOUGH

COCONUT BUNS

Take favorite bun or bread recipe and make the dough a bit sticky. Then form into rolls and roll in coconut. Let rise and bake at 375° until nicely browned, approximately 30-35 minutes. Has a delightful taste.

BAKED APPLES

Take whole apples, core and stuff the center with dates, raisins, brown sugar and spices (coriander and/or anise) and wrap in bread dough that has been rolled out about 1/4-1/2 inch thick. Let rise for 10-15 minutes. Bake at 350° for 45 minutes. Warm up before serving.

CRESCENTS

Roll out dough into circles about 1/4 inch thick. Cut circles into wedges 2 1/2-3 inches across at wide end. Starting with end, roll up each toward point. Place point side down on greased cookie sheet. Curve ends to form crescent. Bake 20-30 minutes at 350°.

DATE ROLLS

Roll dough out evenly 1/2 inch thick. Spread with DATE BUTTER. Sprinkle with nuts. Roll up and cut into slices. Place on greased cookie sheet. Let rise 30 minutes. Bake at 350° for 30 minutes.
Variation: Can sprinkle brown sugar, raisins and anise on rolled out dough instead.

DATE BUTTER

2 c. dates
2 c. water
1 tsp. lemon juice or other flavoring such as vanilla extract
pinch of salt

Mix together and cook over medium heat until dates are cooked to mush. Blend smooth all ingredients.

FRUIT RING

Using favorite bread dough, make approximately 30 balls about 1 1/2 inches in size. Use 10 inch tube pan well greased. Sprinkle chopped dates, nuts and pitted canned cherries over the bottom. Dip dough balls into a mixture of 3/4 c. honey and 3/4 c. juice from cherries. Arrange balls in tube pan, sprinkling fruit mixture of pitted canned cherries, 1 c. chopped dried fruit and 3/4 c. chopped nuts or coconut, between layers. If any juice mixture is left over pour over the top. Let rise in warm place until double. Bake at 350° for about 1 hour. Turn out on serving plate.

PLUM OR APRICOT BALLS

Pit fresh plums or apricots and stuff with a date. Roll out dough 1/4 inch thick. Cut into rectangles about size of recipe card, depending on size of fruit. Wrap around stuffed plum/apricot. Let rise on cookie sheet. Bake at 350° for 1/2 hour or more. Try rolling wrapped fruit in coconut before baking.

FRUIT BREAD

In large bowl cut up 4 c. dried fruit such as raisins, dates, prunes, apricots, cherries, pears, currants. Add 2 c. chopped nuts, such a walnuts, 2 Tbs. grated ORANGE RIND, 1 Tbs. spices such as anise and/or coriander, 1 Tbs. vanilla, 2 c. fresh peeled and cut apples. Mix together and add enough dough for two loaves - dough is at pan stage. With hands knead and mix into dough all fruit mixture. Shape into 3-4 loaves. Place in pans. Let rise and bake at 350° for 45-50 minutes.

SESAME SEED BUNS

Use basic bread recipe. Form into buns and dip in sesame seeds.

COBBLER BISCUITS

Use favorite bread dough recipe. Prepare to pan stage. Roll out 1 inch thick and cut in circles. Place biscuits over hot thickened fruit in a casserole, then let rise for 25-30 minutes. Bake at 350° for 35 minutes. When done remove from oven and push biscuits down into fruit juice so they remain soft.

CLOVER LEAF BUNS

Use basic bread dough recipe. Oil muffin tins. For each clover leaf bun roll three balls the size of cherries. Place into muffin tins. Let rise. Bake 350° for 25-30 minutes.

DANISH SWEET ROLLS

1 Tbs. yeast
1/4 c. warm water
1 Tbs. brown sugar
2 1/2 c. hot water
1/3 c. brown sugar
1 Tbs. salt
1 c. oats
1/2 c. wheat germ
3 c. whole wheat flour
4 c. unbleached white flour

Dissolve first three ingredients and let bubble 10 minutes. Add remaining ingredients. Make bread dough as usual. Punch down after first rising of about 1 hour. Roll out in three sections. Sprinkle on 2 Tbs. brown sugar. Combine 1/3 c. raisins, nuts and anise. Spread on dough. Roll as jelly roll. Shape in ring and place on round baking dish. Cut every 2-3 inches almost to center around ring. Cover and let rise 50 minutes. Bake 350° for 35 minutes.

CORNMEAL BUNS

2 c. cornmeal
4 c. boiling water
1/4 c. honey
maple and vanilla flavoring, optional
1 1/2 Tbs. salt
1/3 c. molasses
1 c. walnuts, optional, ground dry in blender
1 c. warm water
2 Tbs. yeast
1 Tbs. honey
10-12 c. mixture of whole wheat and unbleached white flour

Mix first seven ingredients together in bowl. Cool until warm and add risen yeast mixture made of next three ingredients. Then add enough whole wheat flour and white flour to make soft dough. Knead and let rise in greased bowl

225

until double. Shape into buns, place on greased cookie sheets and let rise until double. Bake in 350° oven for 1/2 hour or more.

Note: Dough may seem to be a little sticky so grease hands.

POCKET BREAD

Using favorite bread dough recipe mix and knead the dough. Divide into balls the size of walnuts and roll into a 1/8 inch thick circle. Place on clean cloth and let rise 1/2 hour. Preheat oven to 400°. Put a few pocket breads on a cooling rack at a time and put in oven. Now watch through the glass as it rises. Bake just a few minutes until just begins to turn golden. Not crispy hard. Take out and put in a basket lined with clean towel. Cover until ready to serve. Kids love to help make these.

BAGELS PART 1

2 Tbs. yeast
3 3/4 c. whole wheat flour
1 1/2 c. lukewarm water
3 Tbs. honey
1 1/2 tsp. salt
1/2 chopped onion, optional
1 Tbs. chives
1 tsp. sweet basil or any salad herb of your choice

Combine yeast and 3 c. flour. Combine water, honey and salt. Add to yeast mixture. Beat at low speed for 2 minutes, scraping sides constantly. Add remaining ingredients. Beat three minutes at high speed. Add enough of remaining flour to make a moderately stiff dough. Knead 5-8 minutes. Let rise 15 minutes. Cut into 12 portions. Shape into smooth balls. Punch a hole with floured finger into center. Pull gently to enlarge hole. Cover, let rise 10 minutes.

Variation: Could replace 1/2 c. water with tomato juice.

PART 2

1 gal. water
1 Tbs. honey

Put water and honey in large kettle. Bring to boil. Reduce heat to simmer. Drop in bagels four at a time for 7 minutes turning once. Drain and place on ungreased cookie sheet. Bake 375° for 30-40 minutes.

QUICK BREADS

COCONUT CRISP CRACKERS

2 c. coconut, ground dry in blender
1 c. unbleached white flour
1 c. whole wheat flour
1 tsp. maple flavoring
1 c. water
1/2 tsp. salt

Mix dry ingredients together. Add water and flavoring. Roll out as thin as possible on cookie sheet. Cut into square. Bake at 350° until golden brown, about 15 minutes. Watch carefully.

YUMMY CRACKERS

3 1/2 c. oats, ground dry in blender
1 c. almonds, ground dry in blender
3/4 c. whole wheat flour
3/4 c. white flour
1 c. coconut, ground dry in blender
1 c. water, more if necessary
2 Tbs. honey
2 Tbs. peanut butter
1 tsp. vanilla
1 tsp. salt

Mix first five ingredients together. Combine the remaining ingredients in blender. Add to dry ingredients. Mix and roll out onto floured board very thinly. Cut crackers with cookie cutters or jar ring and put on greased cookie sheet. Bake at 400° until light brown. Approximately 10 minutes.

CORN CRACKERS OR CHIPS

1 1/4 c. water
1 Tbs. coconut
1 1/2 Tbs. sesame seeds
1/4 c. cashews or coconut
1/4 c. oats or barley flakes
1 tsp. salt
1/2 c. water
3/4 c. oatmeal
3/4 c. oats or barley flakes
onion and garlic powder, optional

Blend first six ingredients well then add remaining ingredients and blend again. Pour small amount into greased muffin tins in middle. Tip from side to side to spread evenly, quite thin. Bake at 350° until golden brown, approximately 5-8 minutes. As batter sits in bowl, it gets thicker, add a little bit of water from time to time. I always have an extra pan ready so I can keep an assembly line going to make it go faster. If you are having them the next day just reheat in a pan for a few minutes to crispen.

CORN TORTILLAS

1 c. cornmeal
1 c. boiling water
2-2 1/2 c. whole wheat flour
1 tsp. salt

Pour the boiling water over the cornmeal. Let stand five minutes. Mix salt and flour. Add enough flour to the cornmeal mixture to make a kneadable soft dough. Knead five minutes. Let sit five minutes. Pinch off a piece of dough the size of a golf ball. Roll out on a floured board in the shape of a circle about four inches in diameter. Cook on an unoiled hot griddle or in a skillet, about two minutes on each side.

WHOLE WHEAT TORTILLAS

2 c. whole wheat flour
1/2 c. white flour
3/4 c. hot water
1/2 tsp. salt
1/4 c. applesauce

Mix flours together. Combine hot water, salt and applesauce. Add the liquid to the dry. Mix well. Divide dough into small balls, roll thin, fry on ungreased skillet.

WHOLE WHEAT GEMS

4 c. whole wheat flour
1/2 c. nuts, ground dry in blender
1 1/2 tsp. salt
2 tsp. vanilla or maple flavoring
1 c. dates or raisins

Mix ingredients together. Add enough water to make consistency of a soft cookie dough, 2-2 1/2 cups. Drop into hot, oiled gem pans by spoonfuls. Bake at 400° until brown, approximately 25 minutes.
Variation: Substitute oats blended to a flour or whole wheat pastry flour for the same amount of whole wheat flour.

CORN DODGERS

2 c. water
1/4 c. raisins or dates
1 tsp. salt
2 tsp. nut butter, may use almonds ground in blender
2 Tbs. sesame seeds, ground dry in blender
1/4 c. soy flour
1/4 c. fine coconut
1 1/2-2 c. cornmeal

Blend raisins with water. Combine all ingredients and using as electric mixer, beat well. Adjust the cornmeal to make soft batter. Heat a heavy pan such as cast iron pan or corn gem pan. Sprinkle cornmeal in bottom or grease. Spoon in batter and bake immediately at 400° for 35 minutes.

BREAKFAST BREAD

1/2 c. warm water
1 Tbs. honey
2 Tbs. yeast
1 c. warm water
3 Tbs. honey
1 tsp. salt
1 1/2 tsp. vanilla or maple flavoring
3/4 c. chopped dried fruit
2 1/4 c. chopped fresh or canned fruit

Dissolve first three ingredients and let set 10 minutes. Add next four ingredients. In oiled 8 x 12 pan place fruit ingredients. Spread dough over fruit and let rise 20 minutes. Bake at 350° for 35 minutes. Cool on rack, fruit side up. Top with roasted nuts.

APPLE BURRITOS

8 apples, peeled and cored
1/3 c. water
1/4 c. dates, chopped
1/4 c. raisins
1/8 tsp. maple flavoring
1/2 tsp. vanilla

Cook apples and dates in water until soft. Add remaining ingredients. Mix well. Roll in tortilla shell and place in baking dish. Cover with glaze. Bake at 350° for 30-40 minutes.

GLAZE

2 c. apple juice
2 Tbs. cornstarch or arrowroot powder
1/2 tsp. lemon juice
1/4 tsp. coriander, optional
1/8 tsp. cardamon, optional

Mix ingredients together and cook over medium heat until lightly thickened. Use on waffles or crepes. May use frozen concentrate, undiluted, for apple juice.

CORN BREAD OR MUFFINS

1 c. cornmeal
1 1/2 c. white flour
1/2 tsp. salt
1/2 c. very warm water
1 Tbs. yeast
2 Tbs. honey
3/4 c. milk, such as soy or tofu milk

Sift first three ingredients together. Mix next three ingredients and let stand until bubbly. Add yeast mixture to flour mixture adding in milk. Pour into greased muffin tins or 9 x 9 pan. Let rise approximately 10 minutes. Bake at 350° until done, about 45 minutes.

Variation: 1/2 c. FLAX SEED JELL can replace 1/2 c. of liquid.

BLUEBERRY MUFFINS

1/2 c. water
1 Tbs. honey
2 Tbs. yeast
1 1/4 c. water
1/2 c. honey
1/2 tsp. vanilla
1 tsp. salt
1 1/2-2 c. unbleached white flour
1 1/2 c. whole wheat flour
2 c. warm blueberries
1/2 c. chopped walnuts

Dissolve first three ingredients in small bowl and let set 10 minutes. Mix remaining water, honey, vanilla and salt in separate bowl. Fold in whole wheat flour and warm blueberries and nuts. Put into greased muffin tins. Let rise 10 minutes. Bake at 350° for 35 minutes.

BRAN MUFFINS

1/2 c. water
1 Tbs. honey
2 Tbs. yeast
1 1/4 c. boiling water
1/4-1/2 c. honey
1/2 c. molasses
3/4 c. raw wheat bran
1 1/2-2 c. unbleached white flour
1 1/2 c. whole wheat flour, approximately
1 1/2 tsp. salt
1-2 c. raisins or dates
1/2 c. chopped walnuts

Dissolve first three ingredients in small bowl and let set for 10 minutes. Mix boiling water, honey, molasses and bran in separate bowl. Let cool to lukewarm. Mix and fold in unbleached white flour and yeast mixture. Let rise 15-20 minutes. Fold in whole wheat flour, salt, dates and walnuts. Put into greased muffin tins. Let rise 10 minutes, not more. Bake 350° for 35 minutes.

BANANA MUFFINS

1/4 c. warm water
1 tsp. sugar
1 Tbs. yeast
1 c. mashed ripe banana
1 tsp. salt
1/3 c. honey
2 tsp. vanilla
3/4 c. chopped walnuts
2 1/2 c. whole wheat flour

Dissolve first three ingredients together and let stand 5-10 minutes. Mix in remaining ingredients. Beat. Fill greased muffin tins 2/3 full. Let rise 20 minutes. Bake 35 minutes at 350°.
Yield: One dozen muffins.

JAN'S WHEAT GERM MUFFINS

2 1/2 c. wheat germ
1 c. whole wheat flour
1 1/2 c. unbleached white flour
1 c. oat flour
1/4 c. gluten flour
1 1/2 Tbs. soy flour
2 Tbs. yeast
2 tsp. salt
3/4 c. sugar
3 1/2 c. hot water
1 Tbs. vanilla
1 c. raisins
1/4 c. sunflower seeds, optional

Mix all dry ingredients except for raisins and sunflower seeds. Mix wet ingredients. Combine wet and dry ingredients and mix well until it is an elastic texture. Add raisins and sunflower seeds. Put in greased muffin tins. Let rise 10 minutes. Bake at 350° for 15-20 minutes until golden brown.

LEFSA

1 large kettle potatoes
1 1/2 tsp. salt
2 c. flour

Cook potatoes with salt. Cool slightly. Mash potatoes to make 6 c. packed potatoes. Put in bowl and add flour. Mix well. Divide into four balls. Knead one ball at a time. Form into 2 inch wide rolls. Cut 2 1/2 inch pieces off and form ball. Roll out into 1/8 inch thick circles on floured surface. Lift lefsa up loosely and gently with a lefsa stick or flipper. Put on preheated medium hot woodstove, griddle or ungreased fry pan. Lightly brown. Will bubble slightly. Flip and brown on other side. Wrap in tea towel and cover.

DOUGH ON A STICK

whole wheat flour
unbleached flour
cornmeal
salt

Prepare at home equal portions of whole wheat flour, unbleached white flour, and corn meal. Add a little salt.
Campout: Find in the forest big sticks about an inch and a half in diameter and then find skinny sticks, the kind you would use for marshmallows. Put desired amount of flour mixture in bowl. Add enough water to make a dough the consistency of soft bread dough. Take a portion and pat into a thin pancake and stretch it around the big stick, on the top too. Cook in fire until forms a golden brown crust. Don't burn. Pull gently off stick. Now take the smaller stick and poke it through the middle of dough, holding vertically to the fire so the inside will finish baking. Then stuff it with your favorite filler such as peanut butter, jam or honey, beans or tofu wiener. Such fun!

VEGETABLES AND POTATOES

BAKING POTATOES IN THEIR SKINS

Potatoes are most often baked, undoubtedly because that requires the least preparation. Simply scrub them with a vegetable brush and pierce their skins in several places. The holes serve as escape vents for steam that builds up inside the baking potatoes and might burst them.

Sweet potatoes should also be scrubbed before cooking, but they need not be pierced, since they do not produce excessive steam. They create another sort of internal moisture during cooking, however; their starch is converted to sugar syrup, making the vegetables moist and sweet. Since the conversion will not occur if the potatoes reach too high a temperature, they should be baked in an oven heated no higher than 375°. White potatoes, however, may be baked at any temperature from 325-425°.

BAKED POTATOES

Scrub the potatoes, pierce the skins with a fork and bake on an oven rack in a 375° oven, they will take about an hour. To test if done, squeeze each potato, using a pad to protect your hand from a burn. If the potato yields to the pressure, it is cooked through. Gently roll the hot potato on a counter to crumble the flesh inside the skin. With a fork, punch holes in the top of the potato in the shape of a cross. Then hold the potato at both ends and squeeze it until it pops open along the cross to reveal the crumbly flesh.

When making chips, fries, hash browns, scalloped or potato salad it is best to precook potatoes until just done and then thoroughly cool.

STUFFED BAKED POTATOES

Select uniform-sized potatoes. Scrub well. Oil lightly and bake until tender, 1 hour. Cut off top side of potato and remove potato pulp from inside, being careful not to tear skins. Mash potato with a little nut milk. Add chopped parsley and a little salt or dill. Stuff into potato skins. Sprinkle with oil and return to oven to brown.

Variations:
-Mash potatoes with peas.
-Mash potatoes with chopped sauteed onion.
-Sprinkle with paprika.

OVEN POTATO SURPRISE

Mashed potatoes
2-3 c. creamed vegetables

One layer of mashed potatoes followed by the cooked creamed vegetables. Cover with mashed potatoes. Bake at 350° until heated through.

POTATO SALAD

4 c. dice, cooked potatoes
3/4 c. chopped celery
1/2 c. grated carrots
1/4 c. cooked cold peas or corn
1/4 c. chopped cucumbers
1/4 c. chopped pickles
1/4 c. chopped onions
ALMOND-POTATO MAYONNAISE OR TOFU MAYONNAISE
1-2 Tbs. MUSTARD

Add seasonings to taste such as onion and garlic powder, dilllweed, basil, salt.

Mix all ingredients together. Line pretty glass bowl with lettuce leaves. Put in potato salad. Decorate with tomato wedges and sprinkle with paprika.

SCALLOPED POTATOES

6 c. sliced precooked potatoes
1 medium size onion
1 c. almonds, blanched
4 c. water
1 tsp. salt
1/4 c. flour
PIMENTO CHEESE SAUCE

Cook potatoes. Cool and slice. Chop onion and saute slightly. Place in baking dish in layers. Blend smooth almonds, salt and flour with 1 1/2 c. water. Add remaining water. Bring to boil. Pour over potatoes. Top with PIMENTO CHEESE SAUCE and bake at 350° until set, about 30 minutes.

TILLY'S POTATOES

12 cold, cooked potatoes grated on large grater
1 small, finely grated onion
1/2 c. cashews
3/4 c. water
Salt to taste

Grate potatoes in large grater. Finely chop onions. Blend smooth remaining ingredients. Mix all together well. Put in oiled casserole. Sprinkle with paprika. Cover and bake in oven at 350° for 45 minutes.

RICE POTATOES

Cook potatoes until thoroughly done but not mushy. Put through potato ricer. A nice change. Serve immediately for they cool quickly.

POTATO CHIPS/FRENCH FRIES

Cut up cooked potatoes to desired thickness. Grease cookie sheets and spread out on one layer. Salt if desired and put in preheated oven at 400°. Bake until crispy brown. Turn and bake if necessary on other side.
Variation: May slice 10 raw potatoes. Toss with 1 Tbs. olive oil and 1 tsp. salt. Place in greased cookie sheet. Bake 35 minutes at 400°. Flip potatoes when lightly browned, after about 20 minutes.

HASH BROWNS, FRIED

Dice cold, precooked potatoes. Using a nonstick skillet lightly grease and put in cut up potatoes. May add a little CHICKEN STYLE SEASONING and garlic salt if you wish. Fry until crispy.

FALL GARDEN MEDLEY

1 onion, sliced and separated in rings
1 green pepper, sliced in sticks
1 5-6 inch cabbage, shredded
1-3 c. canned tomatoes, chopped with juice
1 can pitted black olives, sliced
1/2 c. toasted sesame seeds
garlic powder or granulated garlic to taste
TOFU SOUR CREAM

Place vegetables in layers in large pan with lid. Sprinkle sesame seeds over the top. Simmer until tender. Toss and serve with Tofu Sour Cream. Serve warm or chill and serve.

GOLDEN CARROTS

4 c. sliced raw carrots
1/2 tsp. salt
1 1/2 c. water
2 1/2 c. pineapple chunks
2 Tbs. cornstarch
1/4 tsp. salt

Cook carrots until tender in 1 1/2 c. water with the 1/2 tsp. salt. Drain, reserving 1 cup of the water in which the carrots were cooked. Drain pineapple chunks, reserving juice. Stir salt and cornstarch into the two liquids. In a small pot, cook cornstarch mixture until it thickens and bubbles. Mix carrots and pineapple chunks in a serving dish and pour sauce over. Serve.

BAKED SQUASH

Squash
1/2-1 c. plain nut cream
garlic
salt
seasoning salt

Blend smooth equal amounts of almonds or cashews with water to make a nut cream. Peel squash and cut in cubes. Cook until tender. Put squash in bowl and add nut cream. Then add seasonings to taste. Beat with electric beater until smooth and creamy. Put in baking dish. Bake until heated through.

CREAMED GREEN BEANS

1 quart cooked, drained green beans
2 c. water, or liquid from beans
1/2 tsp. salt
1 tsp. onion powder
1/8 tsp. garlic, powdered or granulated
paprika
1/2 c. cashews or almonds
toasted bread crumbs
yeast flakes, optional

Blend smooth all but green beans, bread crumbs and yeast flakes, with 1 cup water. Add remaining water to blender. Empty into sauce pan. Lightly boil, stirring until mixture thickens. Add green beans. Place in serving dish. Sprinkle top with toasted crumbs and yeast flakes.

Variations: Add onion rings or use sauce for creamed potatoes, peas, cauliflower or other vegetables or put slivered almonds throughout.

PARSNIP BALLS

2 c. cooked, mashed parsnips
1/4 c. almonds, ground dry in blender
1 tsp. salt
1/2 c. chopped celery
1 c. chopped onions
1 c. dry bread crumbs

Combine 1/2 of bread crumbs and rest of ingredients. Form dough into balls and roll in remaining bread crumbs. Arrange on oiled cookie sheet and bake at 375° for 30 minutes.

CREAMED CORN

Hint: When we freeze corn we do the following and everyone loves it.
 Blanch corn on the cob. Cool. Take an ordinary kitchen fork. File the prongs sharp on the ends. Slit kernels along the cob lengthwise. Scrape cob with knife. The result is creamed corn. Freeze.

BEETS HAWAIIAN STYLE

2 c. beets, cooked and cut
2/3 c. water
1 tsp. honey
1/4 tsp. salt
1 tsp. cornstarch
1 Tbs. water
2 Tbs. lemon juice
1 c. pineapple chunks

Combine first four ingredients and bring to boil. Dissolve cornstarch into the 1 Tbs. water. Add to beets. Continue to lightly boil 1 minute. Remove from heat and add lemon juice and pineapple. Serve hot or cold.

CARROT RING WITH GREEN PEAS

1 1/4 c. water
1 tsp. salt
6 c. shredded carrots
1/3 c. onion, chopped
3 Tbs. water
yeast flakes, optional

Bring water and salt to boil in saucepan. Add carrots. Cover pan, reduce heat and simmer about 10 minutes or until carrots are just tender and water is absorbed. Remove pan from heat. Saute onion in water and nutritional yeast. Add to cooked carrots. Spoon mixture into oiled ring mold. Pack in firmly. Bake at 325° for 40 minutes. Remove from oven, cool 3 minutes. Cut around edges with knife and turn out onto serving dish. Fill center with cooked peas. Garnish with parsley sprigs.

PINEAPPLED YAMS

Fill a casserole dish with cooked or canned yams
2 c. pineapple juice
2 Tbs. cornstarch
1/2 tsp. salt

Dissolve cornstarch in juice and salt. Bring to boil stirring constantly. Boil until clear. Pour pineapple mixture over yams. Top with pineapple rings and a maraschino cherry in the middle of each ring. Bake at 350° about 45 minutes or until heated through.

MARINATED ONION SLICES

Slice enough onions to make up 4 packed cups.
Mix:
1 c. lemon juice, fresh is best
1/2 c. honey
1 tsp. salt

Pour over onions and put into enclosed container so you can shake it once in awhile. You may add some mild herbs such as fresh dill, celery salt, thyme. Refrigerate overnight.

THE CABBAGE FAMILY

Cabbage plants produce crisp, pungent vegetables, but the vegetables come from different parts of the plants. Head cabbages are the red, green and savoy varieties as well as their miniature version, brussel sprouts. Brussel sprouts are the tightly rolled leaves of the plant. Cylindrical Chinese cabbages are more loosely packed leaves. With Kohlrabi (german for cabbageturnip), the bulbous plant stem is the part used. Broccoli consists of green buds on a fleshy stalk; and a cauliflower head actually is a compressed flower.

Most cabbages are available the year round. Kohlrabi, however, is most plentiful in summer and fall.

How to shop: Good round-headed cabbages, including brussels sprouts, appear tightly curled; they feel hard and weighty for their size. Their outer leaves are opaque and their cores white, not yellow-a sign of age. A cauliflower should be an unblemished, snow or cream white and its florets should be tightly pressed together. Kohlrabi is young and tender when the bulb diameter is less than 3 inches.

Storing: Do not wash cabbages before storage-extra moisture will hasten decay. If you wrap cabbages in perforated plastic bags for storage in the refrigerator, they will keep for weeks.

Preparation: All cabbages should be washed and trimmed just before cooking. Cut off the exposed stem of Chinese cabbage; slice head cabbage in half and cut out the tough, wedge-shaped inner stem. Save the core to eat raw. Then shred the leaves of both cabbage types for boiling or steaming. When trimming red cabbage, use a stainless-steel knife, the pigment in red cabbage interacts chemically with carbon steel and turns the leaves an unappetizing blue.

For brussels sprouts, remove the loose outer leaves. Cauliflower may be kept whole if you remove its tough stem, but it will cook more quickly if you separate it into florets. Broccoli should be divided into florets and the stems peeled to ensure that they cook as quickly as the tender buds. Either slice the stems into 2 inch pieces or make several shallow, lengthwise slits in whole, peeled stems. Kohlrabi need only to be scrubbed or peeled; its leaves can be cooked with the bulb to intensify its flavor.

Only kohlrabi and Chinese cabbage however, are mild tasting. The other cabbages are relatively strong flavored and become sulfurous in cooking. The rule is keep the cooking time brief and, when boiling or steaming them, use celery leaves or seeds in the pot to tone down their odor.

SALADS

CRANBERRY SALAD

1 orange
1/2 lemon
1 can cranberry sauce, whole berries
1 c. crushed, drained pineapple

Chop orange and lemon. Combine all ingredients and chill.

POTATO SALAD

4 c. diced, cooked potatoes
3/4 c. chopped celery
1/2 c. grated carrots
1/4 c. cooked cold peas or corn
1/4 c. chopped cucumbers
1/4 c. chopped pickles
1/4 c. chopped onions
*Add seasoning to taste such as onion and garlic powder, dill
    weed, basil*
Salt to taste
2 Tbs. LO CAL MUSTARD
ALMOND-POTATO MAYONNAISE OR TOFU MAYONNAISE

Line pretty glass bowl with lettuce leaves. Mix ingredients altogether. Put in potato salad. Decorate with tomato wedges and sprinkle with paprika.

PARSLEY SALAD

1 1/2 bunches parsley
2 tomatoes, diced
1/2 cucumber, not peeled, chopped
1/2 c. sunflower seeds
1 tsp. salt
2 Tbs. lemon juice
2 Tbs. honey

Chop leaves and ends of parsley and add remaining ingredients. Mix and refrigerate overnight to marinate.

GISELE'S GREEK SALAD

1 large onion
1 green pepper
1-2 tomatoes
1 cucumber
1/2 head cauliflower
1/3-1/2 head lettuce, optional
12 olives
GREEK SALAD DRESSING
Chop ingredients. Rub a large wooden salad bowl with garlic. Add all ingredients and toss. Add the following dressing.

GREEK SALAD DRESSING

1/4 c. water
1 Tbs. olive oil, optional
1/3 c. lemon juice
2 Tbs. honey
Vegie Salt

Blend well. Add to salad. Let set 30-60 minutes. Serve with PARMESAN CHEESE.

GREEK PASTA SALAD

1 1/4 c. pasta, spirals, shells or macaroni
1/2 c. green onions, chopped
1 6-oz. can pitted black olives, halved
1-2 cloves garlic, minced
2 tsp. sweet basil
1 tsp. celery seed
salt to taste
1 Tbs. lemon juice
1/3 c. MAYONNAISE, choose from index

Cook pasta until tender and drain well. Add and toss remaining ingredients. Refrigerate 2-3 hours. Toss and serve. Garnish with carrot curls.

ITALIAN (MACARONI) SALAD

2 c. cooked macaroni
1/4 c. chopped olives
1 c. shredded carrots
1/4 c. grated onion
1 c. green peas
ALMOND-POTATO MAYONNAISE or TOFU MAYONNAISE

The green peas may be raw or cooked. Mix all ingredients. Serve on lettuce leaf.

CABBAGE SALAD

Chopped cabbage
1 c. shredded carrot
1 c. unsweetened crushed pineapple
1/2 c. nuts
Salt to taste
MAYONNAISE, choose from index

Mix well. Serve.

CARROT SALAD

2 carrots, shredded fine
1/2 c. celery, or boc choy, chopped
1/4 c. walnuts chopped or 1/4 c. coconut
1/4 c. crushed pineapple and raisins
1/4 c. MAYONNAISE, choose from index

Mix well. Serve.

FOUR BEAN SALAD

2 c. kidney beans, cooked
2 c. garbanzo beans, cooked
2 c. green beans, cooked
2 c. wax beans, cooked
1/2 c. sliced olives
1 c. diced celery, or more
2 small onions, sliced in rings
1 large green pepper, cut in strips
2 Tbs. pimento, cut in strips
1/2 c. lemon juice
1/2 c. honey
Salt to taste

Drain beans well. Mix all except lemon juice, honey and salt. Whiz these in blender or shake well in jar, pour over all and allow to marinate in refrigerator for 6 hours or overnight.

COUNTRY GARDEN PEA SALAD

2 c. frozen green peas
2 Tbs. minced onion
1/2 c. chopped DILL PICKLE
1 c. diced VELVEETA CHEESE
TOFU MAYONNAISE
1/4 tsp. ground celery seed
Salt to taste

Cook peas 5 minutes then drain and cool. Add remaining ingredients and toss gently. Serve chilled. Garnish with celery leaves.

HOT RICE SALAD

2 c. brown rice
1/2 tsp. salt
5 c. water
1 large tomato, chopped
1 cucumber, chopped
1 c. green onion, chopped
1 small green pepper, chopped
1 avocado, diced
Soy sauce to taste

Bring water and salt to a boil in covered saucepan. Add rice, cover. Lightly boil 1 hour. Do not stir while cooking. Remove from pan. Add remaining ingredients. Garnish with toasted sunflower seeds. Serve warm.

MARINATED VEGI SALAD

15 oz. can whole kernel corn, drained
15 oz. can French style green beans, drained
17 oz. peas, drained
1 c. chopped celery
1 c. chopped raw carrots
1 medium onion, diced
1 small jar pimento for color, optional

Pour dressing over top, stir and refrigerate. Serve chilled.

DEBBIE'S SPECIAL CABBAGE SALAD

1/2 c. peanuts or sunflower seeds
1 small cabbage or 1/2 medium head
4 sliced green onions
1 pkg. uncooked Ramen Noodles, without seasoning packet, or
  Chow Mein Noodles

Shred cabbage and add the onions. Mix in any kind of dressing and refrigerate. Crumble the dry, uncooked Ramen or Chow Mein noodles, combine with peanuts and set aside. Just before serving, mix all ingredients together.

GREEN BEAN-BEET SALAD

3 c. cooked, drained green beans
3 c. cooked, coarsely shredded beets
1/4 c. honey
1/4 c. lemon juice
1/2 tsp. salt

Stir together honey, lemon juice and salt. May add other seasonings if desired such as onion powder, parsley flakes, garlic powder. Mix all ingredients and let stand, stirring occasionally to marinate well.

BROCCOLI/CAULIFLOWER SALAD

2 c. broccoli pieces
2 c. cauliflower pieces
2 c. celery pieces
2 c. carrots, sliced diagonally, thin
2 small onions, sliced in rings

Dressing:
1/2-2/3 c. lemon juice
1/2 c. honey
Salt to taste
any herbs you like

Mix vegetables all together. Whiz dressing ingredients in blender and pour over vegetables and put in container with lid. Refrigerate overnight. Shake several times. Before serving add 1-2 c. Tiny Tim tomatoes. So pretty and delightful.

CUCUMBER SALAD

1 c. fresh lemon juice
1/2 c. honey
1/2 tsp. salt
4 c. sliced cucumbers
1/2 c. thinly sliced sweet onions
2 Tbs. finely minced parsley

Mix together first three ingredients. Pour over salad items and toss. Refrigerate for a few hours stirring occasionally.

FRUIT SALADS

WALDORF SALAD

Apples, cubed
Walnuts, chopped
Raisins

Cream:
1 part cashews
2 parts water
honey, vanilla to taste
dash salt

Blend cream well and add to salad.

FRUIT SALAD DELIGHT

1 1/8 c. Emes flavored gelatin, choose desired flavor
1 1/2 c. boiling water
1 qt. peaches
1 20-oz can pineapple chunks or crushed pineapple
1 c. oranges, diced

Dissolve gelatin in boiling water. Drain juice of the fruit into 4 c. measuring cup. Add enough cold water to juice to make total of 2 1/2 cups of liquid. Add to dissolved jello. Cool and pour over fruit and refrigerate.

FRUIT SALAD

Use enough of the following fruits to serve your size of family:
Apples, chopped
Bananas, sliced
Blueberries or strawberries
Sliced peaches, canned or frozen

Blend 1/2 amount of peaches with 1 banana and a dash of honey for a sauce to be mixed into fruit. May add nut cream or PEAR CREAM if desired.

TROPICAL ISLE DELIGHT SALAD

2 apples
2 oranges
2 bananas
1 c. pineapple, drained
1 Tbs. honey, optional
3/4 c. dates, chopped
1 c. flaked coconut

Dice and toss first three ingredients. Add the remaining ingredients. Refrigerate 2 hours before serving. Garnish with slivered almonds. Serve with whole wheat rolls.

THANKSGIVING SALAD

2 c. diced, tart red apples
1 c. chopped nuts
1 c. diced celery
1/2 c. raisins or diced pitted dates
3/4 c. TOFU MAYONNAISE
1-2 Tbs. LO CAL MUSTARD
6 lettuce cups

Mix together all ingredients except lettuce. Serve on lettuce cup.

JELLO SALADS

DELUXE STRAWBERRY JELLO

1 c. Emes strawberry flavored gelatin
1 1/2 c. boiling water
3 c. frozen strawberries

Dissolve gelatin into boiling water. Thaw berries, blend and strain to make 2 1/2 c. of juice. May need to add a little water. Add juice to jello. Stir and chill. Save the remaining pulp if you desire.
Variation: May use any other fruit such as raspberries.

FRUIT SALAD DELIGHT

1 1/8 c. Emes flavored gelatin, choose desired flavor
1 1/2 c. boiling water
1 qt. peaches
1 20-oz. can pineapple chunks or crushed pineapple
1 c. oranges, diced

Dissolve gelatin in boiling water. Drain juice of the fruit into 4 c. measuring cup. Add enough cold water to juice to make total of 2 1/2 cups of liquid. Add to dissolved jello. Cool and pour over fruit and refrigerate.

DESSERTS

At one time desserts were only for the rich and even then they were limited to holidays and festal occasions. Now some feel cheated if the meal is not settled down with something sweet and sticky. In fact sugar consumption has increased 200% since the turn of the century. Our national average is around 40 teaspoons of sugar a day for every man, woman and child. Sugar is added to everything from soup to nuts literally, and not only our teeth are aching, but also our body's immune system is compromised and our ability to ward off the flu and colds isn't what it should be. Look at the labels on your packed food specials and you'll see words like sucrose, dextrose, glucose, lactose, maltose, fructose, honey, corn syrup and molasses-all different forms of sugar, and sugar clogs the system. Americans are consuming more soda pop than water and a twelve-ounce serving contains between nine and twelve teaspoons of sugar.

What can we do about this terror that is undermining the health of our families and especially our children? There are books and pamphlets without number pointing out the problem; warnings are issued by government and health agencies. Even the dentists raise concern over our uncontrollable addiction to sweets. All these efforts are undeniably commendable, but the use of sugar is still on the increase. The place to begin is with something better.

A good unhurried breakfast composed of whole grains that supply the body's need for energy is a good beginning. Avoid the tendency to snack between meals. The body works much better when the meals are regular and nothing is taken in between. Provide a hearty lunch with as much of the fresh vegetables, soups, patties or other wholesome foods as you would enjoy. Eat a small supper mainly from the easily digested types of foods like fruits and grains. If you make your own desserts, you will find that your family will enjoy the pleasure of sharing them together and you will be aware of how much sweetener you are using. It is a wonderful talent to make foods that are nutritious, delicious and avoid the pitfalls that are leading us down the road to ruin. There is a wonderful satisfaction to be gained from simple natural foods that cannot be had from the more complex refined varieties, and your health will be better as well.

COOKIES

CAROB CHIP COOKIES #1

1 1/2 c. coconut butter, recipe is in instructions
2-3 tsp. vanilla
1 tsp. salt
3/4-1 c. honey
1 c. flour
3/4-1 c. carob chips
3/4 c. coconut
2-3 c. rolled oats

For Coconut Butter blend coconut and enough water to make thick spread. Must blend until very smooth. Cream together first four ingredients. Mix in flour then add remaining ingredients. Let set for about 10 minutes for oats to absorb moisture. Drop by spoonfuls on oiled cookie sheet. Flatten slightly and bake at 350° for 20-25 minutes.
Variation: Add any amount of chopped dried fruit, such as papaya or pineapple.

CAROB CHIP COOKIES #2

1 1/4 c. walnuts
2/3 c. water
1/2 c. brown sugar
1 tsp. vanilla
3/4 tsp. salt
1 1/4 c. flour
1/3 c. FLAX SEED JELL
2/3 c. carob chips
1/3 c. chopped nuts

Blend smooth nuts and water. Add to blender sugar, vanilla and salt. Empty blended ingredients into bowl. Stir in flour and FLAX SEED JELL, then add carob and nuts. Drop by spoonfuls onto oiled cookie sheet. Bake at 350° for 30 minutes.

SHORTBREAD CRUMBLES

1 c. flour, whole wheat pastry, white or whole wheat and white
  combined
1/2 c. cornstarch
1/2 c. sugar
1/2 tsp. salt
1 c. almond or cashew butter, commercial or made in
  Champion Juicer
1/2 c. carob chips, optional
1/2 c. dried fruit, optional

Mix all ingredients together cutting in the nut butter last. If too crumbly add a small amount of water to moisten, the more water added, the tougher the cookies. Press into an oiled 8 x 12 pan. Bake at 350° for 30 minutes.

PEANUT BUTTER COOKIES

3/4 c. peanut butter
1/4 c. honey
1/4 c. brown sugar
1/4 tsp. salt
1 Tbs. vanilla
2/3 c. flour
1/4 c. wheat germ or flour

Cream first five ingredients together. Mix in flour and wheat germ. Form balls, flatten with fork and bake at 350° for 10-15 minutes. Watch carefully.

PEANUT BUTTER CAROB CHIP COOKIES

1 c. peanut butter
1 c. SOY BASE, recipe follows
1/2 c. honey
1/4 c. sugar
1/4 c. water
1/4 c. soy or tofu milk powder
2 tsp. vanilla
1/4 tsp. salt
1 c. millet flour or oat flour
2 c. unbleached white flour
2 c. granola
3/4 c. carob chips

Make millet flour by blending uncooked millet in blender or buy millet flour. Make oat flour by blending until fine dry rolled or quick oats or buy oat flour. Cream together first eight ingredients. Mix remaining ingredients. Mix all together well. Roll in walnut sized balls. Put on cookie sheet. Flatten with fork. Bake at 350° for 10-15 minutes. Makes 5 dozen.

SOY BASE

1 c. soy flour
2 c. water

Blend or stir water and soy flour together. Use one of the following methods to cook:
1) Cook in a double boiler for a couple hours until it thickens. Stir occasionally.
2) Cook in crock pot on high, covered, for 3-4 hours. Stir occasionally.
3) Place simmer ring on burner. Place covered saucepan on ring. Lightly boil about 30 minutes. Stir occasionally.
4) Place ingredients in a covered oiled casserole dish. Bake at 350° for 60 minutes. Stir occasionally.
Helpful hint: Make a large quantity at one time. When cool, place in cup or 1/2 cup size portions on a cookie sheet and freeze. When frozen put in plastic bag, and put back in freezer. You now have soy base ready for future use for any recipe that calls for it.

HAYSTACK COOKIES

4 c. unsweetened, shredded coconut
3/4 c. whole wheat flour
1/3 c. rolled oats
3 c. chopped dates
1 1/3 c. chopped walnuts
1 1/2 tsp. salt
1/4 c. honey or orange juice
3/4 c. cold water

Mix together. Scoop onto ungreased cookie sheet with ice cream scoop. Bake until brown, 20-25 minutes, at 350°.

COCO-PEANUT BALLS

2 c. shredded coconut
1/2 c. finely chopped or ground raisins
1/2 c. peanut butter
4 tsp. vanilla or
2 tsp. vanilla and 1 tsp. maple flavoring

Shape into round balls after mixing all ingredients. Chill before serving. May be packed into an oiled flat pan. Cut into squares after chilling.

HONEY MOLASSES CHEWS

1/2 c. honey
1 c. molasses, black strap
1 c. water
1 c. coconut butter, recipe is in instructions
1/2 c. coconut
1 Tbs. vanilla
GRATED ORANGE RIND
1 1/2 tsp. salt
1 Tbs. lemon juice
3 c. flour
1 c. rolled oats

For Coconut Butter: Blend smooth coconut with enough water to make a thick, smooth spread. The 1/2 c. coconut is not part of the coconut butter. Mix all ingredients together. Drop on cookie sheet and bake about 15 minutes at 350°.

CASHEW CRUMBLES

2/3 c. nut butter
1/2 c. cashews, ground dry in blender
3/4 c. honey
3 c. flour, combination of white and whole wheat
1/2 tsp. salt

Mix together. Roll into balls and press a thumb print into center of each. Fill indentation with raspberry jam or other favorite. Bake 10-15 minutes at 350°.

BANANA NUT COOKIES

3 ripe bananas
1/2 c. chopped walnuts
1 c. chopped dates
1/2 c. nut butter
1/4 tsp. vanilla
2 c. rolled oats

Mash bananas and add remaining ingredients. Let stand 15 minutes. Drop on oiled cookie sheet and bake 20-25 minutes at 350°. Cool 5 minutes on pan before removing with pancake turner. Yield 2 dozen.

BARS

BLUEBERRY DELIGHT

Topping:
4 c. frozen blueberries
1 c. raisins
3 Tbs. arrowroot powder

Bars:
1/2 c. honey
1 c. coconut butter, see recipe in instructions
2 c. blended oats
1/2 c. almonds, ground dry in blender
1/2 c. flour
1/2 tsp. salt
1 tsp. vanilla
1/3 c. water or milk, approximately

Cook together, stirring until thickened, the topping ingredients. To mix bar ingredients. Blend coconut with enough water to make a smooth, thick spread. Combine wet and dry ingredients separately then mix together. Add enough liquid to make a crumbly mixture that will pack into a greased pan. Bake at 375° until brown, about 20 minutes. Pour thickened blueberry topping over and sprinkle with coconut. Cool and serve.

POLYNESIAN BARS

Filling:
2 c. chopped dates
4 c. crushed pineapple
3/4 c. water
1 tsp. vanilla

Crumb mixture:
3/4 c. whole wheat flour
3/4 c. unbleached white flour
3/4 tsp. salt
1 1/2 c. quick oats
1 c. nut butter
1/2 c. coconut
1/2 c. chopped nuts

Mix together and cook filling ingredients until dates are soft, about 5 minutes. Mash or blend. Mix together ingredients from crumb mixture. Press half of mixture into a 9 x 13 oiled pan. Spread filling over crumb mixture. Put remaining crumbs on top and pat down well. Bake at 350° for 30-40 minutes. Cool and cut in squares.

GRANOLA BARS

1 c. peanut butter
1/2 c. honey
1/2 c. coconut
1 Tbs. vanilla
3 Tbs. flour
1/4 tsp. salt
4 c. granola

Warm and soften in saucepan first four ingredients. Mix together remaining ingredients. Combine all together. Press into oiled pan and cut. Bake at 350° until brown. Approximately 10-20 minutes.

POPCORN OR PUFFED WHEAT CAKE

1 c. honey
1 Tbs. vanilla
1 c. peanut butter or other roasted nut butter
2 qts. lightly salted popcorn or puffed wheat

Cook first three ingredients until soft ball stage. It will form a ball when dropped in cold water. Quickly pour over popcorn or puffed wheat. Add some whole peanuts, or other nuts, and raisins if desired. Press into greased pans. Cool and slice.

VERNA'S OATMEAL SQUARES

4 c. oats
1 c. coconut
1 1/2 c. whole wheat flour
1 c. brown sugar
1 tsp. salt
2 Tbs. flax seed, optional
1 c. raisins or dates
1 c. chopped nuts
1 c. nut butter
1 c. carob chips, optional

Mix together. You may need a little water to get the right consistency for bars. Pat into oiled pan approximately 1/2 inch thick. Bake for 35 minutes at 350°.

SESAME FINGERS

3 c. raw sesame seeds
1 1/2 c. fine coconut
1/2 c. peanut butter
1/2 c. honey
1/2 c. brown sugar
1 tsp. vanilla
1/2 tsp. salt
1/2 c. chopped nuts
1/2 c. raisins, optional

Mix seeds, coconut, nuts and raisins. Mix together remaining ingredients. Combine. Pat into greased pan 1/2 inch thick. Bake at 300° for 30 minutes or until nicely browned. Slice in fingers 3 inches long. Will stick together when cool.

CAROB FUDGE #1

1 c. dates
1 c. water
1/2 c. carob powder
1/2 c. water
1 c. peanut butter or other nut butter
1 c. chopped walnuts or other nuts
1 tsp. vanilla
2 1/2-3 c. granola, ground dry in blender

Boil dates and water until soft. Blend smooth. Boil carob and 1/2 c. water for three minutes, stirring until smooth. Mix in remaining ingredients. Add enough ground granola to make a bar consistency. Press into greased pan, sprinkle with coconut and freeze. Remove from freezer 1/2 hour before serving. Serve cold or serve directly from freezer.

CAROB FUDGE #2

1/2 c. water
1 c. peanut butter
1 c. DATE BUTTER
1 c. chopped walnuts
1/2 c. carob chips
1/2 c. coconut

Melt carob chips in double boiler on stove. Mix in remaining ingredients. Pat into pan. Chill.

CAROB CLUSTERS

1 c. carob chips
1/2 c. peanut butter
1/4-1/2 c. chopped peanuts or other nuts
2 c. Rice Krispies
1/4-1/2 c. chopped dates, raisins or other dried fruit

Melt carob chips and peanut butter together in double boiler. Mix in your choice of the remaining ingredients quickly and drop by spoonfuls on waxed paper. Or pack into oiled 8x8 pan. Chill before serving. Store in refrigerator or freezer.

HALVAH CAROB BALLS

1 c. sesame seeds
1 c. almonds
1 c. sunflower seeds
1/2 c. honey

Grind first three ingredients one cup at a time in blender. Mix in honey. Form into balls. Dip in melted carob chips. Chill.

CAROB COATED KISSES

1 c. peanut butter
1 c. chopped dates
1/4-1/2 c. honey
1 c. chopped almonds
1 c. roasted wheat germ or ground granola
1/2 c. soy milk powder or 1 c. tofu milk powder
2-3 Tbs. juice or water
2 c. carob chips

Mix all ingredients together with hands except carob chips. Melt carob chips. Dip candy pieces into carob and refrigerate. Store in refrigerator.

MALT TAFFY

3 c. powdered barley malt
1/2 c. water
1/2 c. peanut butter
1/2 c. melted honey
Chopped peanuts and raisins

Mix together and heat on stove stirring constantly, about 5-10 minutes. Add peanuts and raisins. Pour onto greased cookie sheet and freeze. When you wish to serve, just bang and it will quickly break into pieces. Serve immediately and keep remainder refrigerated or it gets soft and hard to pry apart.
Variation: May substitute 3 c. of liquid barley malt. Leave out water. Follow rest of recipe as is.

ALMOST ALMOND ROCA

1/2 c. orange juice
3 Tbs. Minute tapioca
1/4 c. honey
1 c. toasted, finely chopped almonds to be added or just to roll
*   in*
1 c. finely chopped walnuts
1 c. coconut
3 Tbs. carob powder
1 c. ground dates
1 Tbs. vanilla

Cook first three ingredients together. Add remaining ingredients and shape into log pieces. Grind additional almonds and roll in ground almonds. Refrigerate.

CAKES

BOILED RAISIN CAKE

2 c. raisins
3 c. water
1/2 c. warm water
1 Tbs. honey
2 Tbs. active dry yeast
1 3/4 c. raisin water
2/3 c. raw sugar or 1/2 c. honey
1 Tbs. vanilla
1 Tbs. grated ORANGE RIND
1 c. walnuts
1 tsp. salt
1/2 c. whole wheat pastry flour
1 c. additional four, whole wheat or unbleached white
1 1/2 c. unbleached white flour
soaked raisins (these are the 2 c. of raisins called for above)
1 c. chopped walnuts
2 tsp. anise or coriander, optional

Boil raisins and water together for five minutes. Drain off water and save to replace some of the water in recipe. Dissolve yeast and honey in warm water. Blend smooth next seven ingredients in blender. Add to yeast mixture stirring as little as possible. Fold in additional flour and let rise 15-20 minutes, not more. Then fold in remaining flour. Add remaining ingredients. Prepare cake pan by cutting waxed paper to fit, and grease paper or oil and flour cake pan. Fill pan 1/2 full. Let rise in pan 10 minutes, not more. Bake at 350° for 35-40 minutes.

Variations:
#1 - BANANA NUT CAKE

Replace raisins with 2 c. mashed banana. Leave out 3 c. water. Use 1 3/4 c. plain water in blended ingredients. If icing desired, try roasting 2/3 c. nuts, almonds or cashews, and making a thick nut butter. Add some melted honey and vanilla and perhaps orange flavoring or rind. Drizzle over cake before serving.

#2 - Put different dried fruit in batter as well as the raisins, such as papaya and pineapple. Ice with melted carob chips.

FRESH APPLE CAKE

1/2 c. brown sugar
3/4 c. water
1/3 c. nuts
2 tsp. vanilla or 1 tsp. each of vanilla and maple
2 Tbs. lemon juice
2 c. unbleached white flour
2 tsp. health baking powder
1/2 tsp. salt
1 c. nuts, optional
4 c. apples, chopped

Blend smooth first five ingredients. Mix dry ingredients. Stir in with blended mixture. Mix in apples with fingers. Bake in oiled 8 x 10 pan at 350° for 45-50 minutes.

5 MINUTE CAROB CAKE

1 c. nuts of choice
2 c. water
1/3 c. carob powder
1/2 c. FLAX SEED JELL
2 tsp. vanilla
2 tsp. lemon juice
2 c. unbleached white flour
1 c. brown sugar or sucanat
1 Tbs. coffee substitute powder, such as Postum
2 tsp. health baking powder
1 tsp. salt

Blend smooth first three ingredients. Stir blended items with next three ingredients. Mix dry ingredients. Mix all ingredients together. Bake in oiled 8 x 12 pan at 350° for 35-40 minutes. Check with toothpick. After cake is cooled, melt carob chips and spread on cake for icing.

5 MINUTE ORANGE CAKE

2 c. unbleached white flour
1 c. whole wheat flour
1 c. brown sugar or sucanat
2 1/2 tsp. health baking powder
1 tsp. salt
1 1/2 c. soy, tofu or nut milk
1/3 c. orange juice concentrate
2 Tbs. grated ORANGE RIND or 1 1/2 Tbs. freshly grated
    orange rind
2 tsp. lemon juice
2 tsp. vanilla

Mix dry and wet ingredients separately then combine. Bake in oiled 8 x 12 pan or muffin tins at 350° for 35-40 minutes.

GLAZE FOR ORANGE CAKE

1/2 c. orange juice concentrate
2 Tbs. honey
1 Tbs. arrowroot or cornstarch
1/3 c. water
2-3 Tbs. ORANGE RIND or 1 1/2 Tbs. fresh grated orange rind

Melt orange juice in saucepan. Dissolve arrowroot in water and add to orange juice mixture and stir until clear and thickened. Add rind. Spread glaze on cake. Top with finely chopped walnuts if desired.

UPSIDE DOWN CAKE

Filling:
2 c. thickened blueberries
2 Tbs. grated ORANGE RIND or 1 tsp. dried
2/3 c. walnut halves
5-6 shredded apples

Batter:
1 3/4 c. white flour
1/4 c. whole wheat flour
1 Tbs. health baking powder
1/2 tsp. salt
1/4 c. peanut butter
1/4 c. white or brown sugar, date sugar or honey
1 1/4 c. cold water
1/2 tsp. vanilla
1/2 tsp. maple flavoring

Oil an 8 x 12 baking pan. Mix first three items of filling. Pour into baking pan. Next add shredded apples. Bake at 400° for about 15-20 minutes to let apples partially cook. Mix first four ingredients of batter then cut in peanut butter. Add remaining ingredients and mix well. Spread this over apple mixture. Bake at 400° for 35-40 minutes.

WAFFLE CAKE

Filling:
2 1/2 c. boiling water
2 1/2 c. pitted dates
2 peeled apples, quartered
1 c. cashews, ground dry in blender
1/2 c. carob powder
6 Tbs. cornstarch
1/4 tsp. salt
2 tsp. vanilla
1 c. peanut butter, optional

Cake:
waffles
sliced apples
coconut
chopped nuts

Soak dates in water until soft. Mix together all filling ingredients. Blend smooth 1 cup at a time. Pour into saucepan. Lightly boil, stirring, 3 minutes. Chill. Layer waffles with filling and sliced apples if you wish. Garnish with coconut and chopped nuts.

AUNT ANNIE'S PLUM PUDDING

2 c. date sugar, honey or brown sugar
2 c. nut butter, made from Champion Juicer, ie: almond or
*   cashew or commercial nut butter*
1 1/2 lb. bread crumbs, made from 1 1/2 lb. loaf of whole grain
*   bread*
3 c. or 1 lb. currants
6 c. or 2 lb. raisins
2 c. flour
1/2 lb. peeled and cored apples
1/4 oz. mixed Christmas spices
juice of 1 orange
juice of 1 lemon
1 tsp. salt
1 c. fruit juice or milk
1/4 lb. mixed peel
1 1/4 c. FLAX SEED JELL

Cream first two ingredients. Add remaining ingredients and mix well. Grease cans or jars. Line with waxed paper. Fill and steam in canner for nine hours. Serve with favorite sauce. Store in cool place. Makes three plum puddings.

SPECIAL CHRISTMAS CANDY CAKE

1 1/2 c. brown sugar or honey
3 c. sifted white flour
1 tsp. salt
2 c. FLAX SEED JELL
1 Tbs. vanilla
2 tsp. almond flavoring
3 c. or 1 lb. currants
4 c. or 1 lb. soft chopped dates
3 1/2 c. or 1 lb. cherries
3 c. or 1 lb. raisins
3 c. or 1 lb. dried pineapple
3 c. or 1 lb. walnuts or almonds
3 c. or 1 lb. dried papaya

Mix first six ingredients to make batter. Work in remaining ingredients gently with your hands. Heap into four 7-inch loaf pans prepared as follows: cut grocery bags to fit pans and grease well. Bake at 300° for 1 hour, covered lightly with aluminum foil and then 10-20 minutes uncovered. Remove from oven. Peel off liner as soon as cool enough to handle. Let cool. Wrap in waxed paper, then aluminum foil and refrigerate. Keeps all year!

Note: For the lb. of cherries, drizzle some honey on frozen or canned cherries and slow cook for several hours until cooked down but not hard and dry. Or bake in the oven in a glass dish at 250°. You may also use dried cherries. If you don't have dried pineapple, you can use canned pineapple chunks, but they should be cooked in oven the same as cherries.

Variation: May vary dried fruit according to preference and availability.

FLAX SEED JELL

2 c. water
6 Tbs. flax seed

Boil for five minutes. Strain and let cool in refrigerator overnight.

Note: 1/4 c. flax seed jell can be used in place of one egg in some baked goods.

PUMKIN BLACHINDA

Filling:
2/3 c. water
1/2 c. dates
1/2 c. cashews
1/4 c. brown sugar
1 Tbs. cornstarch
1/2 tsp. salt
1/2 tsp. vanilla
1/2 tsp. maple flavor
1 c. cooked pumpkin

Bring water and dates to a boil. Let sit a few min. to soften. Pour in blender. Add remaining ingredients to blender, except pumpkin, and blend smooth. Stir blended ingredients into pumpkin. Put into crust. See recipe below.

PINEAPPLE MINCEMEAT BLACHINDA

Filling:
3 apples
1 c. raisins
1 c. crushed pineapple, drained
1/2 c. applesauce
1/4 c. honey
2 Tbs. orange juice concentrate
1 tsp. lemon juice
1 tsp. coriander
1 tsp. vanilla
1 tsp. maple
1/4 tsp. salt
1 Tbs. GRATED ORANGE RIND, optional

Peel, core, dice apples. Cook with a little water until just barely done. Add remaining ingredients. Bake in crust below.

BLACHINDA CRUST

3 c. coconut
2 1/4 c. water
1 1/2 tsp. salt
1/2 c. raisins
3-5 c. flour of your choice

Mix first 4 ingredients. Blend smooth 1 c. at a time. Pour into bowl. Gradually add flour to make a pie dough consistency. Roll out dough. Use a small bowl or a large jar lid to cut out circles in the dough. Spoon filling into center. Press a second circle over top of first circle and seal with a fork. Bake on an oiled cookie sheet at 350 for 30-40 min. or until golden brown.

LEMON PIE FILLING

3 c. pineapple juice
1/4 tsp. salt
1 c. cashews, optional
1/4 c. brown sugar or honey
1/4 c. cornstarch or arrowroot
1 tsp. grated lemon rind
2 Tbs. lemon juice
1 Tbs. honey

Blend smooth first five ingredients. If using nuts, blend smooth with 1 c. of juice before adding rest of ingredients. Bring to a light boil, stirring until thick. Remove from heat and add remaining ingredients. Put in baked pie shell and chill.

BLUEBERRY PIE

1 pkg., 20 oz. frozen blueberries or 4 c. fresh
1 c. frozen grape juice concentrate, undiluted
1/4 c. quick cooking tapioca
1 1/2 tsp. coconut flavoring or vanilla
1 1/2 tsp. lemon juice
1/8 tsp. salt
1 baked 9 inch pie crust

Thaw blueberries. Mix grape juice concentrate and tapioca and let stand 5 minutes. Bring to a boil; simmer, stirring often, until tapioca is clear, stir in blueberriesand remaining ingredients and let simmer about 5 minutes. Pour into baked pie crust. Refrigerate until firm. Top with favorite cream topping.
Variation: Use as topping for waffles, crepes or cheesecakes. Use only 2 Tbs. of tapioca.

STRAWBERRY PIE

Crust:
1 c. ground granola
1/2 c. coconut
1/2 tsp. salt
Filling:
4 c. frozen strawberries
1-20 oz. can pineapple, crushed or tidbits
1/3 c. honey or sugar, optional
1/4 c. cornstarch (use 1/3 c. cornstarch if using honey)
1 1/2 tsp. vanilla
1/8 tsp. salt

Crust: Mix ingredients. Sprinkle with enough water to beable to pat into oiled 9 inch pie plate. Bake at 375 for 10 min. Let cool before adding filling.
Filling: Thaw and drain strawberries. Drain pineapple. Pour juice from berries and pineapple into saucepan (should be approximately 2 c.). Add remaining ingredients except fruit. Lightly boil, stirring constantly, until thickened. Add fruit. Pour into baked crust. Chill. Variation: May use other frozen fruit in place of strawberries.

CASHEW DATE BANANA TART FILLING

20 pitted dates
1 c. boiling water
2/3 c. cashews
1 c. water
1/2 tsp. salt
1 tsp. vanilla
1 large banana

Add boiling water to dates. Let soften then blend smooth. Pour into saucepan. Blend smooth remaining water with nuts, salt and vanilla. Pour into saucepan. Cook until thick. Slice half banana in bottom of tart shell and pour cooled filling into crust. Top with rest of banana. Chill.

CARROT PIE/TARTS

1 c. dates
3 Tbs. soy flour
2 1/2 Tbs. cornstarch
3/4 tsp. salt
1 tsp. vanilla
1 3/4 c. cooked carrots
1 1/2 c. rich soy, nut or tofu milk

Soften dates in milk. Blend smooth. Add remaining ingredients. Blend smooth. Pour into unbaked pie crust, or tart shells. Bake at 350° for approximately 30 minutes until set. Top with favorite whipped topping.

PUMPKIN PIE

1/2 c. honey
1/4 c. flour
2 c. cooked pumpkin or squash
1/2 tsp. salt
1/2 tsp. vanilla
1 1/2 c. ALMOND MILK, may replace almonds with cashews
1/2 tsp. anise

Blend thoroughly and pour into unbaked pie shell. Bake 450° for 10 minutes and then 325° for 35-40 minutes.

CRUMBLE TOP APPLE PIE

Filling:
1 c. apple juice concentrate
3 Tbs. cornstarch
8 c. peeled, sliced apples
1/4 tsp. salt
1/2 tsp. vanilla
Grated lemon or ORANGE RIND, optional
1 tsp. ground coriander, optional
1/8 tsp. anise flavoring, optional
Crust:
1 c. whole wheat flour
1/4 tsp. salt
1/2 tsp. ground coriander
3/4 c. ground walnuts
1/2 c. quick oats
1/4-1/2 tsp. grated ORANGE RIND
3 Tbs. orange juice concentrate
1 Tbs. water

To make filling, add 1/4 c. apple concentrate to moisten cornstarch; simmer remaining concentrate and apples in saucepan until apples are almost tender. Add cornstarch mixture and simmer, stirring until thickened; stir in seasoning. To make crust, crumble flour, salt, coriander and ground nuts together until texture of fine crumbs. Add oats and toss. Mix wet ingredients together and add to dry, lightly mix together. Save a scant 1/4 of the dough for crumble topping. Press remainder firmly into greased pie plate. Fill with filling. Crumble remaining pastry over the top of fruit; cover fluting with strip of foil lightly pressed over edges. Bake at 350° until topping is light brown and apples are tender, approximately 30 minutes.

Variation: Use this filling for Fruit Crisp or Sweet Roll filling.

CAROB PIE FILLING

3 1/2 c. water
1 c. cashews
1 tsp. vanilla
1/4 tsp. salt
15 dates or 1/2 c. sucanat or brown sugar
1/3 c. cornstarch or arrowroot powder
3 Tbs. carob powder
1 Tbs. coffee substitute powder such as Postum

Blend cashews smooth with 1 c. of water. If using dates, simmer them with 1 c. of water until softened. Blend all ingredients except last 2 c. of water, until smooth. Add water. Bring to boil, stirring constantly until thick. Slice bananas in baked pie crust and pour filling over them. Chill.

Variation: May use 4 c. tofu or soy milk instead of 3 c. water and the nuts.

BASIC PIE CRUST

1 c. quick or rolled oats
2 c. flour (all whole wheat, all white or a combination)
1 tsp. salt
1 c. walnuts
1 c. water

Blend oats until fine to make a flour or buy oat flour. Mix all flour and salt. Blend smooth nuts and water. Combine all ingredients. Add enough cold water to make a soft dough. Roll out on floured board. Fit into oiled pie plates. Bake at 350 for 25-30 min.
Variation: May use all wheat flour in place of oats.

GRANDMA SMITH'S PASTRY

1 1/2 c. quick or rolled oats
1 1/2 c. unbleached white flour
1/2 tsp. salt
1 c. hot water
3/4 c. cashews
1 Tbs. yeast

Blend oats until fine to make a flour or buy oat flour. Mix all flour and salt. Blend smooth nuts and water. Pour into bowl and add yeast. Let rise 10 min. Combine all ingredients. Knead lightly. Roll and fit into oiled pie plates. Bake at 350 for 25-30 min.

CRUMBLE CRUST

1 c. dates and 1/4 c. water OR 1/4 c. honey and 1/2 c. PEAR
  MILK
3/4 c. Grape Nuts
1/2 c. quick oats
3 Tbs. chopped almonds
1/8 tsp. salt

Bring dates and water to a boil. Let sit a few min. to soften. Blend smooth. Or blend together honey and pear milk. Mix remaining ingredients and add to date or honey mixture. Press into oiled 8x8 dish (dampen hands). Reserve 3/4 c. of crust for garnish. Bake at 375 for 10 min. cool and add filling.

GRANOLA CRUST

2 c. ground granola
1 c. ground coconut
1/2 c. flour
2 Tbs. honey
PEAR MILK or water, enough to dampen crust

Pat in oiled 9 inch pie plate or 9x13 baking dish. Bake at 350 for 30 min.

PUDDINGS

MINUTE TAPIOCA

2/3 c. cashews or blanched almonds
3 c. water
1/4 c. honey, brown sugar or date sugar
1/8 tsp. salt
1/4 c. Minute tapioca
1 tsp. vanilla
1 tsp. maple flavoring

Blend smooth nuts, honey and salt with 1 c. water. Add rest of water. Add tapioca and let stand five minutes. Cook over medium heat, stirring constantly until mixture comes to full boil. Pudding will thicken as it cools. Remove from heat. Stir in flavoring. Pour over sliced bananas and raisins in glass bowl. Stir once after 20 minutes. Serve cold.

PEAR TAPIOCA

5 Tbs. Minute tapioca
1/4 c. lemon juice
1 c. pear juice from canned pears
2 c. pineapple juice
5 pear halves, drained

Cook the tapioca with the juices until clear. Let cool five minutes. Pour mixture into individual bowls. Chill. Place a pear half on top of each bowl of pudding.

JANICE'S TAPIOCA PUDDING

3/4 c. quick cooking tapioca
3 c. water
1/8-1/4 c. sugar
1 1/2 Tbs. vanilla
1/2-3/4 c. cashews
3 c. water
1/4 c. tofu or soy milk powder
1 c. coconut, optional
1/2 c. raisins, optional

Cook first two ingredients in microwave, cooking three minutes at a time and stirring. Cook until clear. Takes approximately 15 minutes. While the tapioca is cooking, blend sugar, vanilla, cashews, milk powder with 1 c. water. Add remaining water. Bring to boil and add cooked tapioca and raisins. Chill and serve.
Other options: Sliced bananas, pears, peaches, or any drained fruit stirred in just prior to serving.

Variation: May also cook tapioca on the stove or in covered crock pot.

ORANGE APRICOT PUDDING

Filling:
3 c. hot cooked millet loosely packed into cup
1 c. fruit juice, pineapple, pear, peach, etc.
2 Tbs. vanilla
1/4 c. soy milk powder
1/2 tsp. salt
2 Tbs. sugar
2 Tbs. lemon juice
1 1/2 c. or 1 12-oz. can orange juice concentrate
1/3 c. Emes unflavored gelatin

Crust:
3 c. bread crumbs
1 1/2 c. coconut
1/8 tsp. coriander
2 Tbs. sugar
2 Tbs. flour, scant
1 Tbs. vanilla
1/3 c. applesauce

Apricot Topping:
2 qts. canned apricots
1/3 c. cornstarch
1/2 c. water

Filling: Boil orange juice concentrate then stir in gelatin with fork until dissolved. Add remaining ingredients for the filling. Blend these ingredients until smooth, 1 cup at a time.

Crust: Mix dry ingredients first. Add wet and mix well with hands. Press into bottom of greased 9 x 13 inch pan and bake at 350° until golden brown, approximately 20 minutes.

Topping: Bring apricots to boil. Dissolve cornstarch and water. Use this mixture to thicken the apricots. When cool, pour over the pudding and refrigerate again.

CHEESECAKES

CRUMBLE CRUST

This crust is as well liked as a graham cracker crust.

1 c. pitted dates and 1/4 c. water OR
1/4 c. honey and 1/2 c. PEAR MILK
3/4 c. Grape Nuts
1/2 c. quick oats
3 Tbs. chopped almonds
1/8 tsp. salt

Bring dates and water to boil. Reduce heat to low and simmer, covered, five minutes or until soft. Or blend honey and milk together. Mix remaining ingredients and put in date or honey mixture. Press into oiled 8 x 8 pan using dampened hands. Reserve 3/4 c. for garnish. Bake at 375° for 20 minutes. Cool and add filling.

TOFU CHEESECAKE

2 c. water
1/2 c. flour
1/4 c. honey
1/2 tsp. salt

Blend smooth the above ingredients. Pour into saucepan. Lightly boil, stirring constantly, until thickened. Put half of the cooked mixture back in blender with the following ingredients:

1 1/2 c. tofu
1/4 c. lemon flavored Emes gelatin
1 Tbs. unflavored Emes gelatin
2 tsp. vanilla

Prepare baked crust of your choice or the one below. Pour blended ingredients over crust. Pour in blender remaining ingredients from the saucepan. Add to blender the second group of ingredients (tofu, gelatin, vanilla). Blend smooth. Pour this on top of the previously blended ingredients and crust. Chill. Top with glaze or fruit.

CARMEN'S TROPICAL CHEESE CAKE

Crust:
1 1/2 c. granola
2 Tbs. honey
1 Tbs. water

Cheese filling:
2 c. tofu, drained and crumbled
1 Tbs. lemon juice
1 Tbs. vanilla
1 Tbs. maple flavoring
1 20-oz. can crushed pineapple
2 Tbs. cornstarch or arrowroot powder
1 banana
1/2 c. honey

Filling: Mix filling ingredients together. Blend smooth half of the ingredients. Repeat blending process. Pour the blended ingredients on top of the crust recipe. Bake at 350° for 20-30 minutes until edges are lightly browned and center is firm. Chill.

Crust: Blend granola until fine in blender. Mix crust ingredients together. Press into oiled 8 x 8 baking dish. Bake. Chill. Top with favorite thickened fruit before serving.

KATHY'S TOFU CHEESECAKE

Crust:
1 1/2 c. granola, ground dry in blender
2 Tbs. honey
1 Tbs. water or milk

Cheese filling:
2 c. tofu
1 Tbs. vanilla
1/8 tsp. salt
1/4 c. honey
2 Tbs. water
1 tsp. lemon juice

Mix together crust ingredients and press into bottom of 8 x 8 oiled baking dish. Blend smooth remaining ingredients in blender until smooth, adding a little nut milk, soy or tofu milk to make smooth consistency. Pour over crust and bake at 350° for 30-35 minutes until just lightly browned on top. When cool, top with favorite thickened fruit topping and chill.

DRIED FRUIT BALLS

FRUITY CHEWS

1 c. dates
1 c. dried apricots
1 c. raisins
1 c. pecans or walnuts
1 c. coconut
3 Tbs. lemon juice, fresh is best

Put first four ingredients through a food grinder. Stir in remaining ingredients. Pack smooth in a waxed paper lined pan. Chill and cut into squares. May be rolled in fine coconut. May be made into balls with a walnut flattened into top of ball. Freeze well.

APRICOT YUMMIES

Sun dried unsulphered apricots
Raw walnuts

Mix together equal parts of apricots and walnuts run through course food grinder. Form into balls and roll in coconut.

CAROB DELIGHTS

1 c. granola, ground dry in blender
1/2 c. coconut
1/4 c. carob powder
1/2 c. sunflower seeds, ground dry in blender
1/4 c. sesame seeds, ground dry in blender
1/2 tsp. salt
1/2 c. honey
3 Tbs. peanut butter
vanilla to taste

Heat to soften honey and peanut butter in saucepan. Then combine all the ingredients together and form into balls.

CAROB CANDY

1 c. chopped dates, firmly packed
2/3 c. unsweetened coconut
2/3 c. chopped walnuts
1 1/2 Tbs. carob powder
1 1/2 tsp. vanilla

Mix all ingredients together with you hands, or put through food grinder. Form into balls. Roll in coconut. Store in container in refrigerator.

FRUIT CANDY

2 c. raisins
2 c. walnuts
2 c. chopped dates
1/8 tsp. salt
coconut, optional

Mix and put through food grinder. Make into small balls. May roll in coconut. Store in covered container in refrigerator.

FRUIT SLICE

1 c. figs
1 c. dates
1 c. raisins
1 c. walnuts
1 tsp. orange juice or water
1 Tbs. honey, scant
1/2 c. macaroon coconut

Put dried fruit and nuts through fine food grinder. Stir in orange juice and honey. Mix well, and form into a roll. Roll in the 1/2 c. coconut. Wrap in waxed paper and store in refrigerator.

DATE BALLS

3 c. chopped dates
1 tsp. vanilla
1 c. water
2 c. cereal flakes
1 c. chopped nuts

Simmer first three ingredients stirring constantly until smooth or blend smooth after simmering. Cool and add remaining ingredients. Drop with teaspoon into flaked coconut and roll into balls. Store in refrigerator. Makes 75 balls.

HAWAIIAN TREATS

1 c. coconut
2 c. almond meal
2 c. ground dried pineapple

Place almonds in blender a few at a time to make a meal. Finely blend coconut. Grind pineapple in food grinder. Form into a ball and roll in additional dried coconut. Makes 16 balls.

CAROB ICE CREAM

5 dates
3/4 c. water
1/4 tsp. salt
1/2 c. cashews
2 Tbs. carob powder
1 1/2 tsp. vanilla
4 ripe, frozen bananas

Blend all but bananas smooth. Remove half from blender. Repeat with remaining sauce and bananas. Serve immediately or pour into flat container and freeze. When frozen cut into strips and put through Champion Juicer.

ORANGE ICE CREAM

2 ripe, frozen bananas
2 oranges, peeled, sectioned and frozen
1 c. orange juice
1 c. crushed pineapple with juice
1/4 c. cashews or almonds

Mix all ingredients. Blend half until smooth. Repeat with remaining ingredients. Serve or store in freezer until ready to serve.

VANILLA ICE CREAM #1

2/3 c. cashews
3 1/2 c. water
1 1/2 c. hot cooked millet or rice
1/2 c. honey or 3/4 c. dates
2 tsp. vanilla
1/4 tsp. salt

Blend all ingredients in blender, adding only enough water to blend smooth and thick. When nuts are smoothly blended, add balance of water. Place in hand or electric freezer until stiff, or freeze in ice cube trays then put through Champion Juicer.

Variation: For carob flavor ice cream, add 2 Tbs. carob powder. For maple-nut, add 2 tsp. maple flavoring and pieces of walnut, lightly toasted in oven first if desired. Omit walnuts for maple ice cream.

271

VANILLA ICE CREAM #2

1 c. cashews or blanched almonds
3 c. water
1 tsp. slippery elm powder, optional
1-2 Tbs. soy milk powder
1/2 c. honey
1 Tbs. vanilla
1/4 tsp. salt
1 Tbs. maple flavoring

Blend smooth all but 2 c. water. When smooth, add remaining water. Freeze and put through Champion Juicer or put through ice cream machine as directed.

BRAD'S BLUEBERRY FROZEN DELIGHT

1/4 c. almonds or cashews
2 c. water
1/4 c. raisins or soft dates
1/8 tsp. salt
1-4 frozen banana chunks, according to taste
Frozen blueberries

Blend smooth dried fruit, nuts and salt with 1 c. of water. Add remaining cup of water. Use half of this mixture to blend 1 or 2 bananas and enough blueberries to make desired thickness. Repeat with other half of nut mixture and more bananas and blueberries. Pretty if garnished with coconut.

PEAR ICE CREAM

1 c. cashews or blanched almonds
1 c. water or pear juice
1/4 tsp. salt
1 tsp. vanilla
1/3 c. honey
1 tsp. slippery elm powder, optional
1 qt. canned pears

Blend all but pears until creamy. Gradually add canned pears. Pour into flat covered dish. Freeze. Cut in strips and put through Champion Juicer or blender or food processor. May need to let soften slightly in order to blend.

Variations:
1. Add maple flavoring and walnuts for Maple Walnut.

2. Add 1/2-3/4 c. frozen orange juice concentrate for Orange Sherbet. Add juice concentrate before adding pears.

3. Add 1/2-3/4 c. frozen grape juice concentrate for Grape Sherbet. May leave pears out or add them.

4. Cut the nuts in half and add 1/4 c. tofu or soy milk powder.

5. Add any kind of fruit such as pineapple or strawberries for different flavors.

CASHEW MILK FOR SMOOTHIES

Milk for Smoothies:
1/2 c. water
1/2 c. cashews
1 Tbs. vanilla
2 Tbs. honey
1 1/2 c. water

Smoothies:
1 1/2 c. smoothie milk
8 large frozen strawberries, blueberries or other fruit
Frozen banana pieces

Milk: Blend water and cashews. Add next three ingredients and blend well.

Smoothie: Add frozen fruit to milk until thick.

275

-PATTIES

Big Macs	75
Fish Sticks	73
Millet Meat Balls	85
Millet Patties	79
Oat Burgers	87
Shamburgers	81
Soy Oat Patties	77
Walnut Burgers	83

-RICE

Cabbage Rolls	131
Chow Mein's Chinese Food	135
Curry	141
Hawaiian Rice	137
Spinach Bake	133
Stroganoff	139

GRAVIES

Almond Gravy	209
Cashew Gravy	209
Mary's Brown Gravy	208
Onion Gravy	209

JAMS

Apple Butter	201
Apricot Jam	200
Cera Jel Jam	200
Date Butter	224
Dried Fruit Jam	201
Grandma's Raspberry Jam #1	199
Grandma's Raspberry Jam #2	199
Grape Jam	199
Nut Raisin Spread	201
Pineapple Prune Jam	201
Strawberry Jam	200
Tropical Fruit Spread	199

LITTLE THINGS THAT COUNT

Butterfly Sandwiches	189
Carob Rice Cakes	189
Christmas Nuts & Bolts	190
Frozen Grapes	190
Fruit Leather	189
Gluten Jerky	181
Gopher Pockets	189
Stuffed Dates	189
Trail Mix	190

MAYONNAISE & DRESSINGS

Almond Potato Mayonnaise	202
Avocado Dressing	204
French Dressing	204
Jan's Mayonnaise	203
Pear Cream	204
Sesame Dressing	203
Soy Cashew Mayonnaise	202
Soy Mayonnaise	203
Tarter Sauce	73
Thousand Island Dressing	204
Tofu Mayonnaise	202
Tropical Dressing	204

MILKS

Almond Milk	195
Millet Milk	195
Pear Milk	195

MISCELLANEOUS

Chicken Style Seasoning	213
Cranberry Sauce	212
Curry Powder	213
Flax Seed Jell	259
Jan's Vegetable Seasoning Mix	213
Ketchup	212
Lo-Cal Mustard	211
Orange Rind	212
Soy Sauce	212
Soy Base	248
Spring Rhubarb	39
Sprouts	213
Stewed Prunes	212

SALADS

Broccoli/Cauliflower Salad	243
Cabbage Salad	240
Carrot Salad	241
Country Garden Pea Salad	241
Cranberry Salad	239
Cucumber Salad	243
Debbie's Special Cabbage Salad	242
Four Bean Salad	241
Gisele's Greek Salad	241
Greek Pasta Salad	240
Green Bean-Beet Salad	242
Hot Rice Salad	242
Italian Macaroni Salad	240
Marinated Vegi Salad	242
Parsley Salad	239
Potato Salad	239

SALADS-FRUIT

Deluxe Strawberry Jello	245
Fruit Salad	244
Fruit Salad Delight	245
Thanksgiving Salad	244
Tropical Isle Delight Salad	244
Waldorf Salad	243

SANDWICHES

Bonanza Bean Dip	208
Chicken Salad Sandwich	155
Chicken Style Luncheon Meat	151
Eggless Salad Sandwiches	167
Grilled Cheese Sandwiches #1&2	163
Hommus Tahini	157
June's Heritage Sandwich Spread	149
Nuteena Like Spread	157
Pizza Pockets	161
Super Sandwich Soymeat Slices	165

SAUCES & CREAMS

Apple Syrup	198
Blueberry Orange Sauce	197

Coconut Cream	196
Cranberry Sauce	212
Cream Topping	196
Maple Syrup	197
Millet Sauce	196
Orange Date Syrup	197
Pear Cream #1 & #2	196
Spaghetti Sauce for Pizza	173
Spring Rhubarb	39
Strawberries & Crushed Pineapple	197
Strawberry Yogurt	197

SOUPS

Borscht #1	153
Borscht #2	153
Cauliflower Soup	157
Corn Chowder	155
Cream of Potato Soup	167
Eileen's Favorite Cucumber Soup	165
Frenchies Tomato Soup	151
Lentil Soup	161
Split Pea Chowder	159
Split Pea Soup	159
Tomato Rice Soup	131
Tomato Vegetable Soup	149
Vegetable Lima Bean Soup	163

VEGETABLES

Baked Potatoes	232
Beets-Hawaiian Style	236
Carrot Ring	237
Corn in Bonfire	181
Creamed Corn	236
Creamed Green Beans	235
Fall Garden Medley	234
French Fries	234
Golden Carrots	235
Hash Browns	234
Marinated Onion Slices	237
Oven Potato Surprise	233
Parsnip Balls	236
Pineappled Yams	237
Potato Chips	234
Potato Salad	233
Rice Potatoes	234
Roasted Potatoes	181
Scalloped Potatoes	233
Squash	235
Stir Fry Vegetables	135
Stuffed Potatoes	233
Tilly's Potatoes	234

279

280

281

OTHER FINE BOOKS AVAILABLE FROM FAMILY HEALTH PUBLICATIONS

VEGETARIAN COOKBOOKS

TASTE AND SEE: ALLERGY RELIEF COOKING / Penny King	11.95
OF THESE YE MAY FREELY EAT / Jo Ann Rachor	2.95
OF THESE YE MAY FREELY EAT SUPPLEMENT: PRACTICAL INSTRUCTION IN COOKING AND NUTRITION Jo Ann Rachor	2.95
THE COUNTRY LIFE VEGETARIAN COOKBOOK	9.95
RECIPES FROM THE WEIMAR KITCHEN / Weimar Institute	9.95
THE JOY OF COOKING NATURALLY / Peggy Dameron	9.95
COOKING WITH NATURAL FOODS / Muriel Beltz	14.95
COOKING WITH NATURAL FOODS II / Muriel Beltz	14.95
EAT FOR STRENGTH / Agatha Thrash, M.D.	7.95
EAT FOR STRENGTH (Oil Free Edition) / Agatha Thrash, M.D.	7.95
COUNTRY KITCHEN COLLECTION / Silver Hills Institute	11.95
TEN TALENTS / Hurd	16.95
100% VEGETARIAN: EATING NATURALLY FROM YOUR GROCERY STORE / Julianne Pickle	5.95
STRICT VEGETARIAN COOKBOOK / Lorine Tadej	7.95

NATURAL REMEDIES, LIFESTYLE, NUTRITION ETC.

NUTRITION FOR VEGETARIANS / Agatha & Calvin Thrash, M.D.	9.95
HOME REMEDIES / Agatha & Calvin Thrash, M.D.	9.95
NATURAL REMEDIES / Austin, Thrash & Thrash, M.D.	6.95
MORE NATURAL REMEDIES / Austin, Thrash & Thrash, M.D.	6.95
FOOD ALLERGIES MADE SIMPLE / Austin, Thrash & Thrash, M.D.	4.95
PRESCRIPTION: CHARCOAL / Agatha & Calvin Thrash, M.D.	6.95
FATIGUE: CAUSES, TREATMENT AND PREVENTION / Austin, Thrash & Thrash, M.D.	4.95
ANIMAL CONNECTION / Agatha & Calvin Thrash, M.D.	4.95
PMS: PREMENSTRUAL SYNDROME / Agatha & Calvin Thrash, M.D.	2.95
NEW START / Vernon Foster, M.D.	9.95
HOME MADE HEALTH / Raymond & Dorothy Moore	11.95
GARLIC FOR HEALTH / Dr. Benjamin Lau	3.95
NATURAL HEALTHCARE FOR YOUR CHILD / Austin, Thrash & Thrash	9.95
HYDROTHERAPY: / Clarence Dail M.D., Charles Thomas Ph. D.	8.95
CASE AGAINST COFFEE AND OTHER BROWN DRINKS / Agatha & Calvin Thrash, M.D.	2.50

Order From:

Family Health Publications
8777 E. Musgrove Hwy.
Sunfield, MI 48890

Subtotal _____
Mi Residents
(4% Sales Tax) _____

Shipping:
  $2.00 First Book
  .50 Each Addl. _____

Total Amt. Encl._____